New Directions for Institutional Research

Paul D. Umbach
EDITOR-IN-CHIEF

J. Fredericks Volkwein
ASSOCIATE EDITOR

MW01591062

Benchmarking in Institutional Research

Gary D. Levy
Nicolas A. Valcik
EDITORS

Number 156 • Winter 2012
Jossey-Bass
San Francisco

BENCHMARKING IN INSTITUTIONAL RESEARCH
Gary D. Levy and Nicolas A. Valcik (eds.)
New Directions for Institutional Research, no. 156
Paul D. Umbach, Editor-in-Chief

NEW DIRECTIONS FOR INSTITUTIONAL RESEARCH (ISSN 0271-0579, electronic ISSN 1536-075X) is part of The Jossey-Bass Higher and Adult Education Series and is published quarterly by Wiley Subscription Services, Inc., A Wiley Company, at Jossey-Bass, One Montgomery Street, Suite 1200, San Francisco, California 94104-4594 (publication number USPS 098-830). Periodicals Postage Paid at San Francisco, California, and at additional mailing offices. POSTMASTER: Send address changes to New Directions for Institutional Research, Jossey-Bass, One Montgomery Street, Suite 1200, San Francisco, California 94104-4594.

INDIVIDUAL SUBSCRIPTION RATE (in USD): $89 per year US/Can/Mex, $113 rest of world; institutional subscription rate: $297 US, $337 Can/Mex, $371 rest of world. Single copy rate: $29. Electronic only–all regions: $89 individual, $297 institutional; Print & Electronic–US: $98 individual, $342 institutional; Print & Electronic–Canada/Mexico: $98 individual, $382 institutional; Print & Electronic–Rest of World: $122 individual, $416 institutional.

EDITORIAL CORRESPONDENCE should be sent to Paul D. Umbach, Leadership, Policy and Adult and Higher Education, North Carolina State University, Poe 300, Box 7801, Raleigh, NC 27695-7801.

New Directions for Institutional Research is indexed in *Academic Search* (EBSCO), *Academic Search Elite* (EBSCO), *Academic Search Premier* (EBSCO), *CIJE: Current Index to Journals in Education* (ERIC), *Contents Pages in Education* (T&F), *EBSCO Professional Development Collection* (EBSCO), *Educational Research Abstracts Online* (T&F), *ERIC Database* (Education Resources Information Center), *Higher Education Abstracts* (Claremont Graduate University), *Multicultural Education Abstracts* (T&F), *Sociology of Education Abstracts* (T&F).

Microfilm copies of issues and chapters are available in 16mm and 35mm, as well as microfiche in 105mm, through University Microfilms, Inc., 300 North Zeeb Road, Ann Arbor, Michigan 48106-1346.

www.josseybass.com

CONTENTS

EDITORS' NOTES

Benchmarking has several different uses and purposes in higher education. Some institutions use benchmarking to gauge performance internally to their own organization in regard to departmental performance. Other organizations use benchmarking to gauge their institution among external entities to improve certain performance measures in relation to a specific goal (such as increase in research expenditures or improving the national ranking of the institution).

The definition that the authors relied on in this volume of *New Directions for Institutional Research* is the following:

> Benchmarking is a strategic and structured approach whereby an organization compares aspects of its processes and/or outcomes to those of another organization or set of organizations to identify opportunities for improvement.

In some of the chapters (Chapters 2, 3, 4, and 5) of this volume, benchmarking is used in assessment work to measure different aspects of the institution's mission. For example, benchmarking can be used to gauge effectiveness of certain aspects of university or college instruction by carrying out assessment surveys from year to year among students or alumni. Several institutions also participate in such services as the National Survey of Student Engagement (NSSE), which provides data on surveyed students that can be utilized for benchmarking to help institutions improve aspects of their organization (NSSE, 2011). This volume shows different aspects of benchmarking from a wide variety of perspectives that institutional research offices can use for strategic planning and institutional research purposes.

Chapter 1 provides a historical context and background to how benchmarking has evolved in its usage in higher education institutions over time. Chapters 2 through 5 delve into how benchmarking can be used internally for institutions. Chapter 2 discusses institutional use of comparative analysis of different processes, results, and procedures to obtain useful metrics that can be used to improve performance for different institutional programs. Chapter 3 discusses how benchmarking is used to assist with enrollment management to attain efficiencies in relation to admissions, enrollment, and financial aid.

Chapter 4 discusses how institutions can use surveys that are completed by different entities as starting points for an external benchmarking. An institution can gauge certain performance indices against peer institutions by comparing similar survey information.

Chapter 5 shows how Sabermetrics is used to assess faculty productivity using common statistical techniques that have been used in baseball to show how they can be applied to higher education.

Chapters 6, 7, and 8 focus primarily on external benchmarking for institutional analysis. Chapters 6 and 8 used different methodologies for selecting peers for their institutions. Chapter 6 relates how institutions can use the Integrated Postsecondary Education Data System (IPEDS) for external benchmarking purposes. It also discusses the advantages of using standardized data to assist in the selection of peer institutions for external benchmarking purposes.

Chapter 7 provides a research project to determine whether or not a top-tier-ranked public institution of higher education's linkage with their host municipality had any impact upon their rankings in *U.S. News and World Report*. The research methodology with the top-tier public institutions was also used to explore the same variables in public "emerging universities" benchmarked against top-tier public institutions. The authors attempted to see if any common characteristics with the linkages could be leveraged to improve their rankings in *U.S. News and World Report*. The research in the end revealed other findings that were not initially anticipated by the authors.

Chapter 8 took a very different approach than that in Chapter 7 by developing a statistical model to assist in determining institutional peers. The authors worked with their system colleagues to implement a strategy of minimizing the number of variables used in the statistical model in order to answer a specific benchmarking question. The authors' goal with this methodology was to use variables that were not integral with one another or weighted, which could skew the results. The authors use a step-by-step process in the chapter to show the reader how their statistical model was developed for the purpose of benchmarking to address a specific research question.

Chapter 9 provides a summary of the volume and takes a look into how benchmarking may be used in higher education in the future.

The editors would like to thank all of the authors and personnel that worked so hard and diligently on this volume. Without researchers and support staff, this volume—and journal series, for that matter—would not be possible.

Gary D. Levy
Nicolas A. Valcik
Editors

NEW DIRECTIONS FOR INSTITUTIONAL RESEARCH • DOI: 10.1002/ir

Reference

NSSE. National Survey of Student Engagement: About NSSE. Retrieved on May 5, 2011, from http://nsse.iub.edu/html/about.cfm.

GARY D. LEVY *is the Associate Provost for Academic Resources & Planning and a professor of psychology for Towson University.*

NICOLAS A. VALCIK *is the Associate Director of the Office of Strategic Planning and Analysis and a clinical assistant professor for the Program of Public Affairs at the University of Texas at Dallas.*

NEW DIRECTIONS FOR INSTITUTIONAL RESEARCH • DOI: 10.1002/ir

1

This chapter introduces the concept of benchmarking and how higher education institutions began to use benchmarking for a variety of purposes.

How Benchmarking and Higher Education Came Together

Gary D. Levy, Sharron L. Ronco

The precise origin of the term *benchmarking* is unknown. However, it may have originated from the ancient Egyptian practice of using the surface of a workbench to make dimensional measurements of an object, from the mark cut into a stone or wall by surveyors measuring the altitude of a tract of land, or by cobblers measuring people's feet for shoes. Whatever its origins, implicit in the concept of benchmarking is the use of standards or references by which other objects or actions can be measured, compared, or judged. Modern commercial benchmarking has now come to refer to the process of identifying the best methods, practices, and processes of an organization and implementing them to improve one's own industry, company, or institution. For the sake of this chapter (and this volume) we define benchmarking as a strategic and structured approach whereby an organization compares aspects of its processes and/or outcomes to those of another organization or set of organizations to identify opportunities for improvement.

The practice of benchmarking in American business is widely considered to have originated in the late 1970's. The literature generally acknowledges Xerox Corporation as the first American business organization to formally apply comprehensive benchmarking techniques. In his seminal book on benchmarking, Camp (1989) a former Xerox employee, described how U.S. businesses, smug in their superiority, were blindsided by the invasion into the U.S. marketplace of less expensive and often

NEW DIRECTIONS FOR INSTITUTIONAL RESEARCH, no. 156, Winter 2012 © Wiley Periodicals, Inc.
Published online in Wiley Online Library (wileyonlinelibrary.com) • DOI: 10.1002/ir.20026

higher-quality Japanese-produced goods. Noting that Americans had no equivalent for the Japanese term *dantotsu*, which means striving to be the "best of the best," Camp speculated that Americans were caught off-guard by always assuming that they *were* the best.

Once Xerox realized that Japanese competitors were able to sell their copiers for about what it was costing Xerox to make its copiers, they undertook a thorough examination of competitors' processes, operation by operation. An application of the lessons learned allowed Xerox to later increase design and production efficiency, resulting in reduced manufacturing costs (Yasin, 2002). The concept soon spread to health care, human resource management, the financial service sector, telecommunications, education, and the aerospace industry (Doerfel and Ruben, 2002; Zairi, 1996). IBM, Motorola, and 3M were also early adopters of benchmarking.

Xerox also led the way in another innovative approach, termed *cross-industry benchmarking*. Xerox looked to L.L. Bean, a non-competitor with superior warehousing operations, to address inefficiencies in its warehousing function. Nissan/Infinity benchmarked against Disney, McDonald's, and Nordstrom as well as Ritz-Carlton to improve their human resources and customer service (Yasin, 2002). Southwest Airlines looked to the pit crew of an Indianapolis 500 race car team, and the staff of a hospital emergency room learned how to get customer information quickly from Domino's Pizza (Epper, 1999).

Before benchmarking, most management processes simply projected future performance from past practices, without consideration of targets or superior functional practices in outside organizations. What was innovative about benchmarking was that it established a structured process of comparison that emphasized practices over metrics (Birnbaum, 2001; Camp, 1989). That an organization might be recognized for process excellence instead of just product or service excellence was a radical concept for many businesses (Spendolini, 1992).

The Quality Movement and Benchmarking

The quality movement in the United States of the 1990s (Mouradian, 2002) ushered in a new emphasis on the use of benchmarking as a tool to gauge and improve organizational quality. Benchmarking, viewed as a process-based means to measure and enhance some aspect of an organization's performance, is a fundamental component and tool used in varied approaches to quality enhancement (Yasin, 2002), including Total Quality Management (TQM), Continuous Quality Improvement (CQI), and the Malcolm Baldrige framework.

Total Quality Management (TQM) arose largely in the 1980s and was based greatly on the works of Deming (1986; also see Seymour, 1993). Benchmarking is often noted as a practice that grew out of the TQM movement (Achtemeier and Simpson, 2005), in part because of increased calls for accountability and performance measurement from federal and state governments. Accordingly, benchmarking processes were viewed as a means to improve performance and delivery of quality to varied "customers" (a term often spurned by those in higher education) and identifying opportunities for improvement and greater efficiency (Shafer and Coate, 1992).

The *Continuous Quality Improvement (CQI)* approach was derived in part from aspects of the TQM model. CQI approaches focus on organizational processes and systems and consistently *improving*, rather than simply maintaining organizational quality. Within CQI, benchmarking processes are used to assess current quality in an organization and to identify targets for future improvements.

Benchmarking was given a boost in 1988 when the United States Congress passed legislation to create the *Malcolm Baldrige National Quality Award* (named after a former Secretary of Commerce) partly as a response to the Japanese government's establishment of the Deming Award to recognize quality in industry, but also to promote U.S. business to enhance their international competitiveness through identification of best practices and improvements in quality. The Baldrige framework set forth guidelines for organizational excellence, and incorporated the benchmarking process as an important award criterion.

In short, the Malcolm Baldrige approach is based on several criteria, or foci, used to move toward performance excellence. These criteria include leadership, strategic planning, customer focus, measurement, analysis, knowledge management (where benchmarking resides), workforce focus, and operations focus (www.nist.gov/baldrige/publications/upload/2011_2012_Education_Criteria.pdf). By the mid-1990s, benchmarking was seen as a winning business strategy, surpassing other techniques of the quality movement (e.g., TQM, CQI, and Business Process Reengineering [BPR]). Apparently, the news spread because by 1997 86 percent of companies claimed to use benchmarking in some form or another (Rigby, 1995).

Benchmarking in Higher Education

Benchmarking was optimistically greeted by higher education in the early 1990s as a positive endeavor that would help overcome resistance to change, provide a structure for external evaluation, and create new networks of communication between institutions (Alstete, 1995). Marchese (1995) included benchmarking on the list of "What's In" in *Change* magazine. In 1996 the Houston-based American Productivity and Quality Center (APQC) began facilitating benchmarking studies in higher education in cooperation with the State Higher Education Executive Officers (SHEEO) and other organizations supporting higher education. At this point, benchmarking—and its focus on measuring performance—was becoming entrenched in many areas of higher education (Achtemeier and Simpson, 2005). In 2001 the University of Wisconsin–Stout became the first Malcolm Baldrige National Quality Award winner in higher education.

Over the past two decades, both the National Association of College and University Business Officers (NACUBO) and the American Council on Education (ACE) have developed awards for higher education institutions based largely on the Baldrige model. Ruben (2007), in association with NACUBO, developed a model titled "Excellence in Higher Education" that is based largely on the Baldrige criteria. More recently, the California State University system embraced this model (calstate.edu/qi/ehe/), along with dozens of individual institutions (Doerfel and Ruben, 2002).

Benchmarking activities in higher education are not limited to the United States, however. Fueled by governmental and public concerns for standards and cost-effectiveness, many nations adopted a range of approaches to higher education benchmarking. Jackson and Lund (2000) describe the substantial performance measurement and benchmarking activities undertaken in the United Kingdom since the 1980s. Similar endeavors are evident in Australia, New Zealand, Canada, Germany, and other European nations (Farquhar, 1998; Lund, 1998; Lund and Jackson, 2000; Massaro, 1998; Schreiterer, 1998). More recently, benchmarking of disciplinary learning outcomes was an integral part of the Bologna Process in an effort to create comparable and compatible quality assurance and academic degree standards across several continents (Adelman, 2009).

Despite the potential benefits, full-scale benchmarking has been undertaken by only a relatively small number of higher education institutions (in one example, Penn State undertook a comprehensive benchmarking process against other Big Ten schools; Secor, 2002). More commonly, institutions seek to improve operations more informally by identifying best practices elsewhere and then attempting to adopt those practices. Most of this activity goes unreported in the literature, and so it is impossible to determine how widespread it is.

Birnbaum (2001) asserted that what ultimately found a home in higher education was not benchmarking at all, but a "half-sibling called *performance indicators* and a kissing cousin called *performance funding.*" With the rush for greater accountability, the thoughtful processes envisioned by the concept of benchmarking were quickly replaced by a lust for quick measurement and data. As attractive as this option may be, the sole use of performance indicators ignores a basic and powerful premise of benchmarking—namely, that what is needed for improvement is to identify the *processes* behind the benchmarks or metrics that can lead to improved performance, subsequently demonstrated by associated benchmarks or metrics.

Types of Benchmarking. Like most practices, benchmarking is actually a collection of approaches and techniques that can be conceptualized as a classification scheme or a continuum of self-evaluation activities (Jackson and Lund, 2000). To begin with, benchmarking can be internally or externally focused. *Internal benchmarking* may be appropriate where similar operations, functions, or activities are performed within the same organization. For colleges and universities, these could be academic, administrative, or student service units and involve processes like admissions, hiring, assessment of student learning, or delivery of online instruction. Internal benchmarking may be an end in itself or the starting point for understanding processes that will be externally benchmarked. See Chapter 2 for a more detailed discussion of internal benchmarking.

External benchmarking seeks best practices outside the organization. In *competitive benchmarking,* the products, services, and process of an organization are compared with those of direct competitors; in comparison, *functional benchmarking* examines similar functions in institutions that are not direct competitors. *Best-in-class* or *generic benchmarking* seeks new and innovative practices across multiple industries to uncover the "best of the best."

Benchmarking can also be categorized by its approach: metric, process, or diagnostic (Yarrow and Prabhu, 1999). Almost all benchmarking in higher education can be characterized as *metric* or *performance benchmarking,* which compares selected indicators or metrics among similar institutions to evaluate relative performances (Smith, Armstrong, and Brown, 1999). *Metric benchmarking* is limited to superficial manifestations of business practices (Doerfel and Ruben, 2002) and is restricted to those characteristics that can be quantified.

Process benchmarking, on the other hand, involves a comprehensive comparison of specific business practices with the intention of identifying those aspects of best practice that can lead to improved performance. Process benchmarking is often time consuming and expensive; few who have set out to do it have capitalized fully on its potential (Bender, 2002; Yarrow and Prabdu, 1999).

Diagnostic benchmarking explores both practice and performance, functioning as a continuous "health check" where practices that need to be changed are identified and improvement approaches are devised (Yarrow and Prabhu, 1999). Diagnostic benchmarking may have found its way into higher education via the continuous improvement processes expected by accreditors to document institutional effectiveness.

Some Applications of Benchmarking in Higher Education. Since the early 1990s, several large and high-profile benchmarking studies have been conducted within higher education (Jackson and Lund, 2000; Shafer and Coate, 1992). Perhaps the best-known benchmarking studies in American higher education are those conducted by NACUBO in the early 1990s (Alstete, 1995; NACUBO, 1995). The overall goals of these studies were to develop a standard set of accepted indicators and benchmarks that can be used to improve operational quality and performance, as well as relevant cost information. The initial and wide-ranging goal of the NACUBO study was to help higher education institutions identify "best practices" across varied core functional areas such as admissions, advancement/development, payroll, and so on. Groundbreaking when it was initiated, many of the data points and calculations that emerged from the NACUBO study are now routine. Moreover, some of the ideas and their financial calculations (e.g., ratios) are now included in many standard Department of Education's National Center of Education Statistics (NCES) Integrated Postsecondary Data Analysis System (IPEDS) reports (www. nacubo.org/Research/Benchmarking_Resources/Data_Resource_Details. html).

Another classic benchmarking study in higher education is the University of Delaware's National Study of Instructional Costs and Productivity (better known as "the Delaware Study"; www.udel.edu/IR/cost/). This study originated in the early 1990s from a need at the University of Delaware to evaluate academic programs to be curtailed during a series of difficult budget years (Middaugh, 1994), but now exists as a means for academic leaders and managers to improve program quality and efficiency. Since then, the study has evolved and grown to where it is now the definitive benchmarking study of instructional costs and productivity (Middaugh, 2001). Results provide opportunities to benchmark both internally (across colleges and departments) as well as externally (across institutions and institutional Carnegie classification).

Seybert, Weed, and Bers (2012) provide a succinct summary of other large higher education benchmarking endeavors that provide useful information for institutional researchers, including the National Community College Benchmark Project (NCCBP), the Voluntary System of Accountability (VSA; www.voluntarysystem.org), the IDEA (Individual Development and Educational Assessment) Center (www.theideacenter.org), and the many peer comparison tools available from the National Center for Education Statistics web page (nces.ed.gov). In addition, EBI (Educational Benchmarking, Inc.; www.webebi.com) also offers a variety of benchmarking endeavors covering many academic (for example, student success, first-year experience, diversity) and non-academic (for example, auxiliary services, residence hall, dining services, student unions) facets of higher education. Seybert and colleagues (2012) also provide a detailed account of the National Community College Benchmark Project (NCCP).

As Seybert and colleagues (2012) note, benchmarking has also been commonly used in survey research. There is a large range of surveys sampling student and faculty perceptions of a variety of items within higher education that provide benchmarking opportunities. Some of the largest of these include the National Survey of Student Engagement (NSSE) and its many offshoots (for example, Faculty Survey of Student Engagement [FSSE], Beginning College Survey of Student Engagement [BCSSE], Community College Survey of Student Engagement [CCSSE]; see nsse.iub. edu/, and ACT's many student surveys [www.act.org/highered]).

Barriers to Benchmarking in Higher Education. Whereas benchmarking has become a staple tool for process improvement in business and industry (Southard and Parente, 2007; Stapenhurst, 2009), examples of full-scale benchmarking in higher education are scarce in the literature. It is not hard to identify reasons why benchmarking has failed to gain traction in higher education.

- *Benchmarking has been co-opted by benchmarks.* The push for accountability and transparency in higher education has created an industry of rankings, ratings, and comparison mechanisms. Institutions can populate dashboards with a vast number of data indicators, and compare these over time within the institution, or against comparison groups by using an increasing number of tools and by joining consortia. As mesmerizing as these data may be, none of it provides information about how the superior performance identified with benchmarks can be achieved. True benchmarking leads to understanding the processes that create best practices and creatively adapting those practices.
- *We are unique (just like everybody else).* American higher education rightly prides itself on its diversity and complexity, as reflected by myriad governing and financing structures, types of students and faculty, nature of curriculum and pedagogy, student life, and many other characteristics. Benchmarking assumes that there are practices or processes in other institutions or organizations, comparable to those in one's own, that are superior and worthy of emulation.

  There is a tendency to consider benchmarking as copying, and a resistance to imposing practices that don't fit with the institution. Rather than copying, benchmarking is identifying and assimilating those aspects of best practice that are good for one's own institution.
- *The higher education environment does not support benchmarking.* Benchmarking was an easier "sell" in business, where motives to improve profitability and gain competitive advantages are naturally embraced and outcomes are simpler to define and measure. Higher education has traditionally resisted characterizing its stakeholders as customers or itself as a business and is notoriously suspicious of rapid change.

  Hoffman and Holzhuter (2012) argue that all of the key components needed to support the benchmarking process—acknowledgment of weaknesses, open and honest communication, readiness and flexibility to implement change—are stymied by the models entrenched in the higher education system.
- *Benchmarking is complex, expensive, and labor intensive.* Practitioners agree that, done correctly, benchmarking requires a significant investment of time and effort. Deciding on the scope of the study, identifying best practice organizations, traveling to those sites, deciding on and

capturing best practices, reporting and disseminating features that can be transferred—these are just some of the considerations for planning a benchmarking study. There are no guarantees of return on investment if the identified best practice ends up being incompatible or even counter-productive with practices in the target institution.

Conclusions

Benchmarking activities in higher education have now been firmly established and accepted, as institutions seek to improve the quality and efficiency of the many activities in which they are engaged. As higher education institutions face the continued challenges of having to produce more with fewer resources along with calls for increased accountability, it is likely that benchmarking and its many related activities and strategies will become more central and commonplace. As this volume demonstrates, higher education has access to a wide variety of tools and vast opportunities for innovation in benchmarking.

References

Achtemeier, S. D., and Simpson, R. D. "Practical Considerations When Using Benchmarking for Accountability in Higher Education." *Innovative Higher Education*, 2005, *30*(2), 117–128.

Adelman, C. *The Bologna Process for U.S. Eyes: Re-learning Higher Education in the Age of Convergence*. Washington, D.C.: Institute for Higher Education Policy, 2009.

Alstete, J. W. *Benchmarking in Higher Education: Adapting Best Practices to Improve Quality*. ASHE-ERIC Higher Education Report, #5, George Washington University, 1995.

Bender, B. E. "Benchmarking as an Administrative Tool for Institutional Leaders." In B. E. Bender and J. H. Schuh (eds.), *Using Benchmarking to Inform Practice in Higher Education*. San Francisco: Jossey-Bass, 2002.

Birnbaum, R. *Management Fads in Higher Education*. San Francisco: Jossey-Bass, 2001.

Camp, R. C. *Benchmarking: The Search for Industry Best Practices That Lead to Superior Performance*. Milwaukee, WI: ASQC Quality Press, 1989.

Deming, W. E. *Out of the Crisis*. Boston: MIT Press, 1986.

Doerfel, M. L., and Ruben, B. D. "Developing More Adaptive, Innovative, and Interactive Organizations." In B. E. Bender and J. H. Schuh (eds.), *Using Benchmarking to Inform Practice in Higher Education*. New Directions for Higher Education (no. 118, pp. 29–38). San Francisco: Jossey-Bass, 2002.

Epper, R. M. "Applying Benchmarking to Higher Education." *Change*, 1999, *31* (November/December), 24–31.

Farquhar. R. "Higher Education Benchmarking in Canada and the United States of America." In A. Schofield (ed.), *Benchmarking in Higher Education: An International Review*. London: CHEMS; Paris: United Nations Educational, Scientific and Cultural Organization, 1998.

Hoffman, A. M., and Holzhuter, J. "Benchmarking." In A. M. Hoffman and S. D. Spangehl (eds.), *Innovations in Higher Education*. Washington, D.C.: American Council on Education, 2012.

Jackson, N., and Lund, H. *Benchmarking in Higher Education*. Buckingham, England: Open University Press, 2000.

Lund, H. "Benchmarking in UK Higher Education." In A. Schofield (ed.), *Benchmarking in Higher Education: An International Review.* London: CHEMS; Paris: United Nations Educational, Scientific and Cultural Organization, 1998.

Lund, H., and Jackson, N. "Benchmarking in Other HE Systems." In N. Jackson and H. Lund (eds.), *Benchmarking in Higher Education.* Buckingham, England: Open University Press, 2000.

Marchese, T. "Understanding Benchmarking." *AAHE Bulletin,* 1995, 47(8), 3–5.

Massaro, V. "Benchmarking in Australian Higher Education." In A. Schofield (ed.), *Benchmarking in Higher Education.* London: CHEMS; Paris: United Nations Educational, Scientific and Cultural Organization, 1998.

Middaugh, M. F. "Interinstitutional Comparison of Instructional Costs and Productivity, by Academic Discipline: A National Study." Paper presented at the Annual Forum of the Association for Institutional Research (AIR), May 1994.

Middaugh, M. F. *Understanding Faculty Productivity: Standards and Benchmarks for Colleges and Universities.* San Francisco: Jossey-Bass, 2001.

Mouradian, G. *The Quality Revolution: A History of the Quality Movement.* Lanham, Md.: University Press of America, Inc., 2002.

National Association of College and University Business Officers (NACUBO). *Benchmarking for Process Improvement in Higher Education.* Washington, D.C.: National Association of College and University Business Officers, 1995.

Rigby, D. K. "Managing the Management Tools." *Engineering Management Review.* Spring, 1995, 88–92.

Ruben, B. D. *Excellence in Higher Education Guide: An Integrated Approach to Assessment, Planning, and Improvement in College and Universities.* Washington, D.C.: National Association of College and University Business Officers, 2007.

Schreiterer, U. "Benchmarking in European Higher Education." In A. Schofield (ed.), *Benchmarking in Higher Education: An International Review.* London: CHEMS; Paris: United Nations Educational, Scientific and Cultural Organization, 1998.

Secor, R. "Penn State Joins the Big Ten and Learns to Benchmark." In B. E. Bender and J. H. Schuh (eds.), *Using Benchmarking to Inform Practice in Higher Education.* New Directions for Higher Education (no. 118, pp. 65–78). San Francisco: Jossey-Bass, 2002.

Seybert, J. A., Weed, E. J., and Bers, T. H. "Benchmarking in Higher Education." In E. Secolsky and D. B. Denison (eds.), *Handbook on Measurement, Assessment, and Evaluation in Higher Education.* New York: Routledge, 2012.

Seymour, D. *On Q: Causing Quality in Higher Education.* Phoenix: Oryx Press, 1993.

Shafer, B. S., and Coate, L. E. "Benchmarking in Higher Education: A Tool for Improving Quality and Reducing Cost." *Business Officer,* 1992, 26(5), 28–35.

Smith, H., Armstrong, M., and Brown, S. (1999). *Benchmark and Threshold Standards in Higher Education.* New York: Routledge.

Southard, P. B., and Parente, D. H. "A Model for International Benchmarking: When and How?" *Benchmarking: An International Journal,* 2007, 14(2), 161–171.

Spendolini, M. J. (1992). *The Benchmarking Book.* New York: AMACOM.

Stapenhurst, T. *The Benchmarking Book: A How-to-Guide to Best Practice for Managers and Practitioners.* Oxford, England: Elsevier Ltd., 2009.

Yarrow, D. J., and Prabhu, V. B. "Collaborating to Compete: Benchmarking Through Regional Partnerships." *Total Quality Management,* 1999, 10, 793–802.

Yasin, M. M. "The Theory and Practice of Benchmarking: Then and Now." *Benchmarking: An International Journal,* 2002, 9(3), 217–243.

Zairi, M. *Effective Benchmarking: Learning from the Best.* London: Chapman and Hall, 1996.

GARY D. LEVY is the Associate Provost for Academic Resources and Planning and a professor of psychology at Towson University.

SHARRON L. RONCO is the Assessment Director for Marquette University.

2

This chapter discusses the application of benchmarking processes within higher education institutions.

Internal Benchmarking for Institutional Effectiveness

Sharron L. Ronco

The real voyage of discovery consists not in seeking new landscapes, but in having new eyes.

—Marcel Proust

Performance benchmarking activities have become ubiquitous in higher education, although what is commonly considered "benchmarking" is really comparative analysis. Using summative metrics to compare one institution's graduation rates, faculty workload, or fiscal indicators with another's has limited utility. It does not identify the practices that result in an institution's superior performance relative to another's, provide solutions to problems, or drive change to achieve better results. The purpose of benchmarking is to identify the *processes* behind the benchmarks that can lead to improved performance and transfer those best practices in a cycle of continuous improvement.

Many organizations have realized significant process improvements and cost benefits through benchmarking. After Camp's (1989) landmark publication on benchmarking at Xerox, the practice accelerated in business and industry, producing a plethora of publications in the 1990s and 2000s. Benchmarking is now practiced on all five continents and has become an established part of business life (Stapenhurst, 2009).

However, the full-scale analysis of operations and activities that underlies effective benchmarking has been uncommon in higher

New Directions for Institutional Research, no. 156, Winter 2012 © Wiley Periodicals, Inc.
Published online in Wiley Online Library (wileyonlinelibrary.com) • DOI: 10.1002/ir.20027

education, or at least uncommonly reported. The American Productivity and Quality Center (APQC) developed a consortium benchmarking methodology in the mid-1990s to facilitate sharing of best practices among groups of institutions with a common interest in improving performance in a certain area. While not developed specifically for benchmarking, the Baldrige Performance Excellence Program (n.d.) offers guidance for assessing processes and outcomes in an educational context. Despite its strong potential, benchmarking has not been widely embraced. It is labor intensive and requires a strong commitment to change and a significant investment of resources (Epper, 1999). Even when institutions cooperate to identify best practices, the discovery that successful processes in one institution are not necessarily transportable to another culture and organizational structure can derail the effort.

An approach that circumvents the difficulties of access, cooperation, comparability, and transferability of processes across institutions is internal benchmarking. Internal benchmarking is the process of identifying, sharing, and using the knowledge and practices within one's own organization (O'Dell and Jackson Grayson, 1998). It assumes that there is variability in the work processes of an organization that has resulted from differences in organizational geography, history, the nature of managers and employees in different units, and so on. By comparing similar operations, functions, or activities within an organization, best practices and opportunities for improvement can be identified within a common environment. Internal benchmarking lowers the stakes inherent in external comparisons and taps the knowledge and best practices already residing within the organization.

Internal benchmarking is an established practice in business and industry for identifying best in-house practices and disseminating the knowledge about those practices to other groups in the organization. A benchmarking leader, Xerox was able to recapture over one-third of its market by comparing administrative and manufacturing processes in its U.S. and Japan operations. Xerox won the Baldrige Award, crediting internal benchmarking for driving the turnaround (Zairi, 1996). O'Dell and Jackson Grayson (1998) point out numerous examples of where internal benchmarking resulted in significant payoffs at companies as diverse as Texas Instruments, Dow Chemical, Chevron, and Kaiser Permanente. Internal benchmarking, while beneficial in its own right, is also regarded as a necessary precursor to benchmarking externally.

Internal Benchmarking in Higher Education

Some years ago, a colleague and I developed an Institutional Effectiveness inventory to identify existing assessment practices and reassure faculty that assessment was not an entirely new and unfamiliar undertaking (Ronco and

NEW DIRECTIONS FOR INSTITUTIONAL RESEARCH • DOI: 10.1002/ir

Brown, 2002). Like many assessment professionals, I characterize assessment of student learning as formalizing and documenting the teaching and learning that is already occurring in classrooms and programs. In similar fashion, many institutions already engage in what is essentially internal benchmarking, without ever calling it that. The difference between anecdotally reporting that Department X does not admit graduate students as efficiently as Department Y, and benchmarking the process of graduate admissions, is the formalization of the comparison. Internal benchmarking objectively locates performance measures, studies processes, and closes the loop by applying transferable aspects of a successful program to others.

Internal benchmarking can be done with structures, processes, outcomes, or even individuals. In colleges or universities with multicampuses or a high degree of devolvement, internal benchmarking compares similar functions or activities across divisions, units, or campuses. Candidate processes for internal benchmarking might include admissions, hiring, assessment of student learning outcomes, approaches to strategic planning, academic and administrative support services, and delivery of online instruction, to name a few.

As is the case with external benchmarking, there are few examples of internal benchmarking in the higher education literature. In an early instance, MBA students undertook a surprisingly well-received project to improve teaching by ranking their faculty and describing why there were differences (Alstete, 1995). Secor (2002) reports how in 1999 Penn State University established teams to investigate and discuss teaching and learning processes across academic departments and identify, gather, and share best pedagogical practices. Marquette University's peer review assessment process sets aside one day each year for academic and cocurricular program assessment leaders to review each other's assessment activities. Discussion is guided by an assessment cycle rubric, but the real value is engaging in dialogue about assessment methods and practices, receiving peer feedback, and generating new ideas. Written peer review forms document progress in developing meaningful assessment, intentionally identifying concepts and strategies that can be adapted by other programs (Bloom, 2010).

Are You Ready to Benchmark?

Theoretically, intra-institutional benchmarking should encounter fewer barriers than cross-institutional comparisons. Data is more accessible and accurate, and transferring practices is likely to be better accepted because of similarity in culture and environment (Southard and Parente, 2007; Stapenhurst, 2009). Goals for improvement seem more realistic when they are already being accomplished elsewhere in the organization. Administrators can avoid threatening overtones by promoting it as organizational learning. Internal benchmarking supports institutional effectiveness and demonstrates a commitment to regional accreditors that the institution is involved in an ongoing process of analyzing information and using results for improvement.

Conversely, organizational structures that promote silo behavior or cultures that do not value or reward learning from others are not prepared to benefit from internal benchmarking. Open internal communication is a key requirement for successful benchmarking. Intra-organizational learning can only take place in an environment where everyone feels free to share information and can see the benefits that can result from it. Benchmarking is by definition a participative exercise that starts with people doing the work, relies on their recommendations and buy-in to change process, and ends with their decision to implement the identified process improvements on an ongoing basis (McNair and Leibfried, 1992).

For successful internal benchmarking to proceed, there must first be an acknowledgment that there are processes that can and should be improved. Second, it is necessary that there be at least two duplicate or similar processes within the organization that can be compared. If a definitive best practice has not yet been identified, there should at least be some indication that superior practices exist and are transferable to others (Southard and Parente, 2007). See Exhibit 2.1 for specifics on conducting an internal benchmarking study.

Initial Steps

Internal benchmarking starts with the identification of critical areas in need of improvement. Many times, an organization is well aware of where its challenges lie. University administrators can usually identify departments whose structures are working effectively as opposed to those in need of restructuring. Other times, customer satisfaction surveys reveal areas where something particularly good is happening, leading to speculation as to how that superior performance can be extended to other areas. For example, does the Institutional Research office have glowing endorsements from its on-campus users while Information Technology struggles with less favorable reviews? Student satisfaction surveys can uncover information about which administrative and academic support services are effective and which may have problems. Student engagement surveys like the National Survey of Student Engagement (NSSE) and the Community College Survey of Student Engagement (CCSSE) may point to effective pedagogical strategies in one department that could be fruitfully adopted by others.

Most institutions maintain departmental metrics on numbers of faculty, faculty to major ratios, retention rates, faculty workload, and research productivity, among others. Although interdisciplinary comparisons are

Exhibit 2.1 Guide to Conducting an Internal Benchmarking Study

Planning the Study

Which processes, practices, or functions will be studied?
What are the purpose, scope, and time frame for the study?
What will be compared? Has a best practice been identified?
Who will conduct the study?
How will information be collected?

Collecting Information

What performance measures are available?
What process information is needed?

Analyzing Information

Can best practice be identified (or confirmed)?
What is the difference between best practice and others?
What makes best practice better than the others?
What are the bottlenecks, problems, and opportunities for improvement?

Implementing Change

How should study findings be communicated and to whom?
Can the best practice be transferred to other areas?
What technique(s) will facilitate successful transfer?
How can success of the transfer be monitored?

not always appropriate, there may be something to be learned from a department that does an unusually good job at retaining majors to graduation, in obtaining external funding, or other areas discovered through metric indicators. O'Dell and Jackson Grayson (1998) caution against letting measurements get in the way, however, and advise focusing on those units where dramatic differences in performance point to a real underlying process difference, and not just an artifact of single-point measurement.

To identify benchmarking potential, Keehley and others (1997) suggest examining areas:

• Where improvement can have significant impact on users and customers
• With high visibility inside the organization
• That consume at least a fair amount of resources, including time
• With a history of problems
• That have potential for improvement and are not constrained by regulations, statutes, and laws
• Not currently undergoing major revision

How to Benchmark

Most benchmarking methodologies, whether internally or externally applied, follow the basic phases introduced by Camp. Organizations typically use anywhere from four to twelve steps in the benchmarking process, which can be summarized as versions of the plan-do-check-act cycle familiar to assessment practitioners.

Planning. Once a process, function, or service is selected for benchmarking, its purpose and scope should be defined. For example, the purpose of benchmarking academic advising processes across a university's colleges or campuses might be to reduce time to degree, improve student satisfaction, prepare information for an upcoming accreditation visit, or perhaps gather evidence in support of an entirely different model for delivering advising services. A clearly defined scope defines what will be studied, and what time and resource boundaries will be placed on the project (Keehley and others, 1997). Making these expectations explicit will keep the benchmarking process on the appropriate level of professionalism and increase the acceptance of its findings.

Generally, benchmarking studies are done by teams rather than undertaken by a single individual. The study team can consist of managers, employees, and customers or stakeholders and is led by a champion or senior advocate. It is critical that the team include representatives from the areas to be benchmarked ("process owners") to ensure that accurate information is collected and to encourage their cooperation in the effort.

Collecting Information. Performance measures are the quantification of how a program, process, or function is operating. Information collection can begin with any existing data indicators that may be relevant to the benchmark study. Institutional researchers may be able to mine their routinely produced data but will typically need to look more deeply for process indicators. For example, a study examining different types of learning communities might begin with collection of data on enrollment, retention, and academic success but would also include indicators relating to their operating conditions and activities. Student or customer satisfaction surveys, including an analysis of written comments, may provide pertinent data for benchmarking as long as the responses indisputably address the specific units under study. Familiar to assessment professionals, well-constructed analytic rubrics are useful scoring guides for measuring performance. In Marquette University's assessment peer review, rubrics are used to evaluate progress in each component of the assessment process. A study investigating which classes produce superior results in "Writing Across the Curriculum" programs might rely on rubrics used to evaluate writing samples.

While performance measures are almost always essential to the benchmarking process, they are usually not sufficient. Metrics do not help other units achieve outstanding results or understand how to do it themselves. In addition, situational variables may be exerting a strong influence on performance measures. Superior results do not always come from a superior process, or conversely, a unit working under adverse circumstances could appear to be producing average results with an outstanding process (O'Dell and Grayson Jackson, 1998).

The investigation into nonquantifiable practices will often become the focal point of the benchmarking study. What are the qualifications of personnel? How does work move through the process? How is the workload distributed? Are physical working conditions a barrier to productivity? How does management operate? Can intangibles like trust, communication, and employee empowerment be deconstructed? Collecting this type of information will usually take the form of interviews or focus groups. It is critical that the institution's leadership create a cultural environment that values sharing, open communication, and a sense that "we are all in this together." This is where benchmarking business operations may be easier than in other areas, since higher education can benefit from the experience of business and industry (Reider, 2002).

Analyzing Information. Quantitative analysis is used to compare metrics from the benchmarked project. Performance gap analysis compares the target or best-practice metrics with those of other participating projects. The analyses are typically presented as data tables, displayed in bar charts, or plotted in radar (spider) charts. The performance gap is the remaining difference after extenuating circumstances have been taken into account; it indicates the potential improvement available to the participants (Stapenhurst, 2009).

Qualitative analysis will require the study team to reflect on the synthesis of evidence bearing on why one practice is better than another, and what makes it so. If a best practice has been previously identified, this is the time to confirm that designation. Care must be exercised when identifying best practices to be absolutely sure that the practice to be held up as "exemplary" really is, or risk demoralizing other units who recognize the shortcomings of the so-called best-practice unit (Bender, 2002). If a best practice cannot be identified by this point, the exercise has not been in vain: The information gained can serve as a springboard to seeking superior practices externally.

Implementing Change. Once the study team summarizes benchmarking findings and communicates them to appropriate audiences, its final responsibility is to develop recommendations for how to bring other units up to best practice standards. Reider (2000) suggests that recommendations coming from the affected units themselves are the ones most likely to be adopted.

The process of transferring best practice has both a cultural and a practical component. Those who have been identified with the best practices may need to be given time and support to serve as coaches for others in the organization. Leadership must provide the resources and remove barriers for those seeking to reach higher standards. An organizational climate that values sharing and transfer can be cultivated by managers who ask regularly what people are learning from others and how they have shared worthy ideas, and reward those who model sharing behavior.

One way to monitor progress and make sure that benchmarking becomes integrated into the ongoing improvement of the organization is through "best practice" teams, composed of managers or professionals with responsibilities at similar levels in similar units. Many institutions already have enrollment management teams, assessment committees, or student affairs committees to fulfill this function. Part of these committees' responsibilities could be to act as internal consultants for each other in sharing processes for carrying out the functions of their individual units. Internal transfer is a people-to-people process; learning and transfer is an interactive, ongoing, and dynamic process; the wellspring of best practices need never run dry (O'Dell and Jackson Grayson, 1998).

Conclusions

Experts agree that the biggest drawback to internal benchmarking is its inward focus: What is lauded as best practice within the institution may fall far short of best practice in other organizations (Elmuti and others, 1997; Southard and Parente, 2007; Stapenhurst, 2009). To expand the learning potential, the experiences gained through internal benchmarking can be a precursor to external benchmarking with peer institutions, with noncompetitors, or even with organizations outside higher education. The process itself can pay dividends in helping break down silo cultures and bridge the gaps that divide organizational units, creating an environment that promotes a culture of learning. At the very least, the institution will have documented its existing processes and activities and established baselines for future comparisons.

All regional accrediting agencies include standards that require higher education institutions to demonstrate a commitment to improvement through systematic evaluations of effectiveness in all areas. Individual units develop their own approaches to this evaluation but seldom look across units to discover what they can learn from each other. Internal benchmarking takes advantage of the experts and expert knowledge already residing within the institution to achieve that effectiveness and demonstrate a commitment to continuous improvement.

References

Alstete, H. (ed.). *Benchmarking in Higher Education: Adapting Best Practices to Improve Quality.* ASHE-ERIC Higher Education Report, no. 24(5), 1995.
Baldrige Performance Excellence Program. "2011–12 Education Criteria for Performance Excellence." Gaitherburg, Md.: n.d. Retrieved November, 2012, from http://www.nist.gov/baldrige/publications/education_criteria.cfm.

Bender, B. E. "Benchmarking as an Administrative Tool for Institutional Leaders." In B. E. Bender and J. H. Schuh (eds.), *Using Benchmarking to Inform Practice in Higher Education*. New Directions for Higher Education (no. 118, pp. 113–120). San Francisco: Jossey-Bass, 2002.

Bloom, M. F. "Peer Review of Program Assessment Efforts: One Strategy, Multiple Gains." *Assessment Update*, 2010, 22(5), 5–8.

Camp, R. *Benchmarking: The Search for Industry Best Practices That Lead to Superior Performance*. Milwaukee, WI: ASQC Quality Press, 1989.

Elmuti, D., and others. "The Benchmarking Process: Assessing Its Value and Limitations." *Industrial Management*, 1997 (July/August), 12–19.

Epper, R. "Applying Benchmarking to Higher Education." *Change*, 1999 (November/December), 24–31.

Keehley, P., and others. *Benchmarking for Best Practices in the Public Sector*. San Francisco: Jossey-Bass, 1997.

McNair, C. J., and Leibfried, K. *Benchmarking: A Tool for Continuous Improvement*. The Coopers & Lybrand Performance Solutions Series. Essex Junction, Vt.: Oliver Wight Publications, 1992.

O'Dell, C., and Jackson Grayson, C. "If Only We Knew What We Know: Identification and Transfer of Internal Best Practices." *California Management Review*, 1998, 40(3), 154–174.

Reider, R. *Benchmarking Strategies: A Tool for Profit Improvement*. New York: John Wiley & Sons, 2000.

Reider, R. "Internal Benchmarking: How to be the Best—and Stay That Way." *Journal of Corporate Accounting and Finance*, 2002, 13(4), 41–48.

Ronco, S., and Brown, S. "Finding the Start Line with an Institutional Effectiveness Inventory." *AIR Professional File*, 2002, 84 (Summer), 1–12.

Secor, R. "Penn State Joins the Big Ten and Learns to Benchmark." In B. E. Bender and J. H. Schuh (eds.), *Using Benchmarking to Inform Practice in Higher Education*. New Directions for Higher Education (no. 118, pp. 65–78). San Francisco: Jossey-Bass, 2002.

Southard, P. B., and Parente, D. H. "A Model for Internal Benchmarking: When and How?" *Benchmarking: An International Journal*, 2007, 14(2), 161–171.

Stapenhurst, T. *The Benchmarking Book: A How-to Guide to Best Practice for Managers and Practitioners*. Oxford, England: Elsevier Ltd., 2009.

Zairi, M. *Effective Benchmarking: Learning From the Best*. London: Chapman & Hall, 1996.

SHARRON L. RONCO is the Assessment Director for Marquette University.

3

This chapter looks at the importance of benchmarking in terms of admissions, enrollment, and financial aid within an organization used to assess enrollment management's performance.

Benchmarking and Enrollment Management

Robert L. Duniway

Every college and university, whether public or private; two-year, four-year, or graduate; traditional or online, depends on recruiting and enrolling new students and strives to have as many of those students as possible complete their educational programs. Knowing how effectively your institution is managing the various stages of enrollment is critical to institutional success, and benchmarks are an important tool for evaluating enrollment management success. This chapter will present a set of benchmarks for evaluating performance at each stage of the enrollment management process, including prospecting, applications received, admit rates, yield, financial aid discounting, retention, graduation rates, academic progress efficiency, and managing course section offerings.

Overview

The work of enrollment management is central to the operation of any college or university. From the standpoint of our educational mission, we can only be successful if we have a population of students reasonably well prepared to succeed in the courses and academic programs we offer. From the standpoint of sustaining the institution, we need the size of the student population to stay within a range where we are neither taxed beyond our capacity to deliver quality instruction and other services nor under-enrolled to the point where we lack the revenue needed to cover operational expenses. The revenue implications of enrollment will depend on the organization of our institution, including the total revenue (net

NEW DIRECTIONS FOR INSTITUTIONAL RESEARCH, no. 156, Winter 2012 © Wiley Periodicals, Inc.
Published online in Wiley Online Library (wileyonlinelibrary.com) • DOI: 10.1002/ir.20028

institutional financial aid) that we receive for each enrolled student and the marginal cost per additional student of providing instruction and other services (Bontrager, 2004; Hossler and others, 1990; Ward, 2005).

With so much at stake, the leaders of any college or university need to regularly evaluate the effectiveness of their enrollment management efforts. In this chapter, I present an overview of key aspects of enrollment management to be watched and suggest sources of benchmarking information which can be used to evaluate local performance in a broader context. I discuss readily available sources of benchmarking information, and note important issues where benchmarking data are either not available or are of uncertain value. I also discuss alternatives to external benchmarking, which can be useful in evaluating an institution's relative level of performance.

Some Notes on Benchmarking

As used in this volume, *benchmarking* refers to systematic comparison of aspects of an organization's performance with the performance of other organizations. For a benchmark to be useful it must address an important aspect of an institution's performance in a meaningful way. This depends both on the meaningfulness of the measure itself and on the relevance of the organizations against which the internal benchmark measure is compared.

Ideally, benchmarks can be developed against a carefully selected set of peer institutions so that differences in performance can't easily be explained away by differences in educational mission, size, governance structure, selectivity, size of endowment, geographic location, or other factors, which do significantly alter what is possible to achieve in enrollment management.

Of course, the ideal is not always available. In some cases, the best that is available are broad reference group measures, perhaps narrowed down by Carnegie classification and/or public or private control. In other cases, institutions voluntarily participate in data sharing, and the institutions we would most like to benchmark against choose not to participate in these exchanges. Following the adage that it is wise not to make the perfect the enemy of the good (Voltaire, 1764), it is more informative to compare institutional performance with benchmarks based on less-than-perfect comparison groups and to carefully consider the ways in which institutional differences may be slanting the results than to not look at comparative data at all.

In a few cases discussed in this chapter, comparison with other institutions is not readily available. If the measure is meaningful but cannot be benchmarked against other institutional results, then how can we evaluate such results in a way that can help identify opportunities to improve performance? Two strategies are available in such cases. We can benchmark internally, comparing results between programs, departments, or schools

NEW DIRECTIONS FOR INSTITUTIONAL RESEARCH • DOI: 10.1002/ir

where we expect consistent results. If the percentage of admitted applicants who enroll is much higher for history majors than for most other humanities programs, but much lower for philosophy majors, then we may want to learn what the former department is doing well and see if there are reforms that could improve the results of the latter. We can also compare current performance to historical performance levels. If in the past we received applications from 15 percent of students who submitted inquiry cards and in the most recent year we received only a 10 percent conversion of inquiry cards to applications, it is worth looking at what changed and how we might return to historical levels of performance.

All of the preceding comments suggest that benchmarking is a means to an end, and not an end in itself. The end is more effective management leading to better performance. Any process through which regular measures of meaningful aspects of performance are evaluated in a context that reveals opportunities to improve future performance is valid and valuable. In the remainder of this chapter, I will suggest ways to construct such a process for improving enrollment management. These suggestions will need to be adapted to the local context at each college or university, but attending to these measures will pay off for any institution where the goal is to educate students in an effective and efficient manner.

Scope of Enrollment Management

Enrollment management encompasses obvious functions, such as admission of new students, retention of continuing students, and student completion of and graduation from academic programs. The literature on enrollment management has focused primarily on the stages of admission and on retention and graduation rates, and these topics will be covered in depth in this chapter. Focusing solely on the longitudinal progress of students through these various stages, however, does not reflect other critical aspects of effective enrollment management. Not just if but also how students are able to progress successfully to graduation is important, and student progress often depends on financial support and always depends on the availability of the classes students need to complete their program requirements. The model for delivering these classes varies between institutions, and this has implications for the maximum enrollment capacity at an institution as well as the resources that will be needed to deliver the appropriate number of course sections. So a complete set of enrollment management benchmarks needs to address admissions, financial aid, student academic progress, and the organization of instructional resources into available classes. Retention and graduation benchmarks may provide an overall score of student success but don't by themselves reveal much about why students are or are not progressing.

Admissions. The stages of the admissions process are frequently described in terms of a funnel. At the top of the funnel are the recruited potential students or prospects. These may be names purchased for mailing campaigns from the College Board or ACT, or the attendees at college fairs or other recruiting events. Some of these prospects respond, asking for information and/or instructions on how to apply. In this chapter those who ask for information are labeled as inquiries. Not all inquiries result in applications, so the number of applications is a smaller group represented further down the funnel. Similarly, in most institutions not every applicant is admitted, so admits are represented as a smaller group even further down the funnel. Of those admitted, a percentage will accept the offer of admission, either by submitting a required deposit or simply by completing a confirmation process to accept the offer of admission. This is the gross yield of admitted applicants. And, sadly, not every student who confirms actually enrolls, so the smallest block at the bottom of the funnel represents those students who actually matriculate (see Figure 3.1).

The rates of transition between various stages of the admission funnel are useful measures of enrollment effectiveness. The response rate from different prospecting activities can be calculated as the percentage of prospects who request information or an application. The percentage of prospects or inquiries submitting an application is the conversion rate. The percentage of applicants who are admitted is the admissions rate. The percentage of admitted applicants who accept admission (deposit or simply confirm) is the gross yield. The percentage of those who accept but ultimately don't matriculate is the melt rate. Finally, the percentage of admitted applicants who enroll is the admissions yield.

Figure 3.1. Admissions Stage Funnel

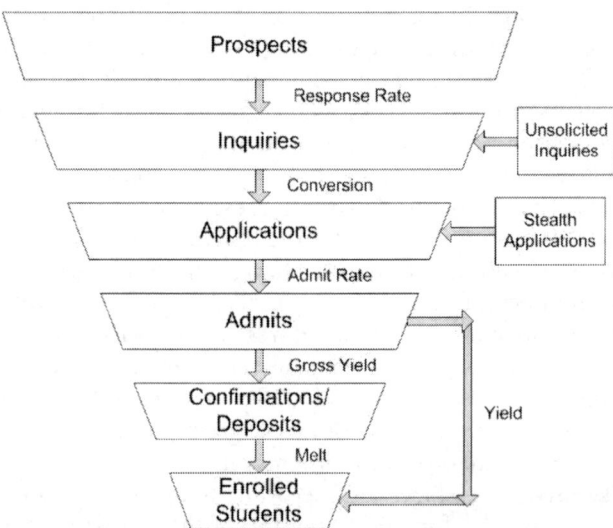

Tracking individuals and calculating these various ratios is relatively straightforward, with three important qualifications. First, it is important to ensure that you are counting individuals only once as an applicant, admitted, and enrolled student for a given admissions funnel even when they submit multiple applications to different programs. If you are evaluating the admissions funnel for all new first-time-in-college (FTIC) undergraduates, a prospect that submits applications for five majors, is offered admission to two of these programs, and accepts and matriculates as a double major is still only one prospect who yielded one matriculated student. Conversely, if you are evaluating the admissions funnel for a particular program, then an applicant who is not admitted into that program but ends up matriculating into a different program shouldn't be counted as enrolled in the program's funnel even though they are enrolled as part of a larger admissions funnel.

Second, when evaluating the overall effectiveness of prospecting activity, it is simple to divide the number of inquiries by the number of prospects, but doing so may be misleading because most colleges receive unsolicited inquiries from students visiting the college website, learning about a college in one of several college guides or online search tools, or learning about the college from family or friends. To gauge the effectiveness of prospecting efforts it is necessary to identify the prospects contacted and calculate the percentage of those prospects that made additional contact with the institution (response rate) or submitted applications (conversion).

Third, a similar issue occurs when the first contact a student makes with a college is to submit an application. Such applications are sometimes referred to as "stealth apps" because they are not on a college's radar until they drop their application. Simply dividing the number of applications by the number of inquires or prospects will overstate the efficiency with which prospects and inquiries are being converted to applications. Again, it is necessary to identify the population of prospects and then to identify what percentage of that population applied to evaluate the efficiency of prospect conversion efforts.

In terms of benchmarking, the FTIC undergraduate admissions rate and yield figures are freely available for any institutions submitting Integrated Postsecondary Education Data System (IPEDS) data.[1] This makes it possible for nearly any institution to identify a set of peer institutions that represent true market competitors and to evaluate how these rates compare.

At the top of the funnel there is not much publicly available information against which to evaluate your institution's performance. The consulting firm Noel-Levitz makes available several benchmark reports for enrollment management at the website www.noellevitz.com/papers-research-higher-education/enrollment-campus-planning/benchmark-reports-higher-education. From this site you can download their

Admissions Funnel Report, which contains information on four-year public and four-year private institutions that agreed to provide data to Noel-Levitz. It is difficult to know how comparable the institutions represented in these figures are to any individual institution, and they do not address two-year college admissions funnel rates. Still, for four-year institutions they provide a point of reference, which may be helpful in interpreting the institution's own admission funnel metrics.

The issue of limited comparison data at the prospect and inquiry end of the funnel may not be a severe limitation in practice. Most institutions engage in a variety of recruiting activities, and the most important question to answer may not be how these strategies fare compared to those employed in the admissions offices of other colleges, but rather which of these strategies provides your institution with the best or worst return on investment. If a careful record is kept of who is contacted in each prospecting effort and of the initial source of student-initiated contact, then it is a simple matter to calculate what percentage of each of these populations converted to an application, was admitted, enrolled, retained, and graduated. Knowing that particular prospecting efforts produce more enrolled students per dollar spent than other efforts may be the most important metric for improving admissions office performance and does not require external benchmark data. Knowing which recruiting efforts produce streams of enrolled students who are most likely to ultimately graduate makes it possible to connect selection of prospecting strategies with educational mission fulfillment.

The cost of prospecting campaigns is one aspect of another important benchmark for an admissions office operation: the cost of recruiting new students. Figures on admissions office costs per enrolled student are available in another Noel-Levitz report, *Cost of Recruiting an Undergraduate Student.* Here, data are available for two-year institutions as well as for public and private four-year institutions.

Beyond the number of students enrolled and the cost of recruiting them, the issue of the quality and composition of each new student cohort needs to be addressed strategically in enrollment management. Different colleges have a variety of goals concerning the populations they hope to serve, so this coverage of entering cohort benchmarks is not intended to be exhaustive, but simply to suggest some common and readily available benchmarks that may speak to the enrollment goals and educational mission of many colleges.

The most commonly available class profile statistics concern gender, race and ethnicity, standardized test scores, high school grades, and/or class standing. In IPEDS, the demographic composition of entering students is readily available for any set of peer institutions completing the mandatory annual report for Title IV financial aid–eligible institutions. IPEDS also makes available SAT and ACT twenty-fifth and seventy-fifth percentile figures, providing one measure of the level of academic preparation of entering students.

Information about high school grades and class rank of entering students is not available through IPEDS. However, this information is collected in the Common Data Set (CDS) used as a common source of data by many college guides. If the peer institutions of interest complete the CDS, you may be able to access a copy of this file from their websites, or obtain the desired information from one of the various college guide sites such as Peterson's or U.S. News.

For institutions committed to providing access to an economically diverse population, one useful benchmark may be the percentage of enrolling students who receive Pell grants. These federal grants are available to high-need students, and thus the percentage of Pell recipients is an indication of the relative proportion of high-need students enrolled at different institutions. This figure is available through IPEDS in the financial aid section.

Financial Aid. Financial aid data are not only useful in enrollment management for providing demographic profile information about the percentage of high-need students enrolled. Financial aid also plays an increasingly critical role in attracting new students and ensuring that students are able to continue on to degree completion. Financial aid can also significantly impact the net financial resources per student available to fund instruction and other services. In thinking about financial aid benchmarks from the perspective of enrollment management, we need to introduce a few key concepts at the individual student budget level, and then consider the cumulative impact of individual student awards on net revenue.

From a student's perspective, what college costs, the net price, equals the total cost of attendance at a particular institution minus the amount of grant and scholarship aid from all sources (federal, state, private, and institutional). Financial aid in the form of student loans or work study awards does not reduce net price, though it may make it easier for students and their families to pay the net price of attending college. Knowing an institution's net price relative to its market competitors is critical in order to understand the value proposition as perceived by potential students. Fortunately, the National Center for Education Statistics (NCES) now makes it easy to access the average net price of peer institutions through the College Navigator website, http://nces.ed.gov/collegenavigator/. In addition, if the mission of an institution includes affordability for students from a variety of income levels, this site also provides average net price for various family income ranges. This can be immensely valuable in understanding how your institution compares to peers in terms of affordability for students from a range of economic backgrounds.

How students cover their net price, in particular how much they rely on borrowing, may also be of concern to enrollment managers, particularly in an era where colleges with high default rates run the risk of losing access to federal student loans. Again, the College Navigator site provides ready access to the percentage of students receiving federal student loans and the average loan amount received for your own and for peer institutions. The CDS provides additional information on debt loads, showing the average cumulative debt at graduation of students who took out loans and the percentage of graduates with loans. College Navigator provides data on student loan default rates for the three most recent cohorts.

Affordability matters in enrollment management because most students report that price and financial aid are important factors in deciding where to enroll. However, students cite academic quality as an even more important factor in selecting a college (Pryor, Hurtado, Saenz, and Korn, 2007), so comparisons of net price are most useful when the comparison institutions enroll students with a similar academic profile. Institutions may buy a better profile through more generous financial aid offers to offset lower academic reputation, but unless the high-ability students thus recruited are offered challenging high-quality classes and degree programs, such a strategy is unlikely to shift the academic reputation of the school, and removal of generous financial aid awards will result in the entering class profile reverting to previous levels (Baum and Schwartz, 1988). If your institution is able to maintain a comparable academic profile with other institutions that have a similar net price, this suggests that potential students view the value of your institution as on par with this peer set. If your institution has a significantly lower net price than similarly selective peers, it suggests either that there is the potential to raise net price and reap more net tuition revenue or else that your institution is not viewed as being of the same academic quality as the comparison institutions and requires a lower net price to attract similarly qualified students.

From an institutional perspective the resources needed to support high-quality educational programs typically come from three sources: spending from endowment earnings and annual gifts to the institution, government (primarily state) subsidies, and net tuition revenue after institutional grant aid. Many institutions, particularly private nonprofit colleges but increasingly public institutions as well, focus on the student discount rate, the percentage of gross tuition revenue given back in institutional grant aid. The National Association of College and University Business Officers (NACUBO) conducts an annual tuition discounting survey and issues a report that institutions can use to benchmark their own discount rate. Institutions that participate in the survey can access this report online at www.nacubo. org/Research/NACUBO_Tuition_Discounting_Study.html. Nonparticipating institutions have the option to purchase the report.

It is also possible to use IPEDS data to approximate the first-time-in-college (FTIC) discount rates of peer institutions. IPEDS data includes the percentage of FTIC students receiving institutional grant aid and the average grant amount of these recipients. Multiplying the average grant times the percentage receiving grants produces the average grant for all FTIC students. Dividing this amount by tuition and fees produces the first year in college discount rate.

The discount rate figure, however, may be less meaningful than simply calculating the average net tuition and fees per student, since a low priced college with a lower discount rate may still have fewer resources per student available to support instruction and other services. Ideally, we would like to know the total revenue from all sources available per student. It is possible to use IPEDS financial data to estimate this amount in one of two ways. One approach is to add the revenue sources of tuition and fees, federal, state, and local appropriations, investment income and gifts, and divide this total by student full-time equivalency (FTE). This approach is imprecise, since some of these funds may go to support operational expenses unrelated to academic program quality.

A second approach is to divide the total instructional costs by student FTE, assuming that institutions have identified resources to cover these expenses through a combination of the revenue categories specified above. The advantage of this approach is that it does not risk counting revenue diverted to other purposes than instruction as available for investing in academic quality. The disadvantage of this approach is that what counts as instructional expense may vary slightly between institutions, and some noninstructional expenses may actually support a high-quality educational experience at many institutions. The limitations for these financial measures may mean that a simpler benchmark such as net tuition revenue per entering student is a more useful measure for private nonprofit institutions. For public institutions, however, appropriations represent a significant proportion of enrollment-based revenue, so some attempt to provide the total revenue picture of the institution and its peers will be necessary to make the measure meaningful.

Student Academic Success. Of course, the goal in higher education is not simply to maximize net tuition revenue. Institutional success occurs only when students successfully complete a set of courses leading to completion of a degree or other educational objective. The most widely used benchmarks for measuring academic success, which are readily available through IPEDS, are the first-to-second-year retention rate and the graduation rate within 150 percent of nominal time to degree.

If students do not return in their second year, they are voting with their feet, indicating either that an institution's programs are not perceived to be of a high enough value to justify the net price they are asked to pay, or else that the student is unable to successfully complete the program. Knowing which of these factors is in play requires a closer look at the academic performance of nonreturners prior to their departure. If a high percentage of nonreturners were behind normal academic progress (earning significantly less than a full-time load's worth of credit if enrolled in a full-time program of study) or were below minimum grade requirements to continue in their chosen program of study, then lack of academic preparation and/or inadequate academic support once they enrolled would seem to account for attrition. If departing students are performing well academically, the cause of attrition is more likely to be that students did not perceive an educational value for the net price they are being asked to pay.

A useful way to confirm or refute such conjecture is to submit a list of students who dropped out before graduation to the National Student Data Clearinghouse matching service. If students who leave are either not showing up at all or are typically enrolling in less selective colleges (often two-year colleges with open admissions standards), this would be consistent with a population of students unable to meet the academic demands of your institution. If students leaving your institution without graduating are regularly showing up in colleges that are as selective or more selective, this suggests dissatisfaction with the value of the education they received for the money they were spending. Students who leave in good academic standing at high-priced institutions and show up enrolled in less expensive (often public) colleges regardless of the academic selectivity of those colleges may simply be unwilling to take on the financial burden necessary to attend your school.

Another way to look at the value proposition, one that directly relates to the investment in providing classes needed for students to complete their programs in a timely manner, is to look at the size of the gaps between on-time graduation and graduation within 150 percent of nominal time to degree. A four-year college that has a comparable six-year graduation rate with similarly priced peer institutions but a lower four-year graduation rate may represent a worse educational value because costs continue into the fifth or even sixth year, and because opportunities provided by graduation are not realized as quickly. If this pattern is coupled with higher average debt loads at graduation, then a college could improve its value to students and its affordability by finding ways to enable more students to complete their degrees on time.

Challenges in Interpretation of Benchmarks

A rich understanding of the key metrics for strategic enrollment management, including admission funnel statistics, retention and graduation rates, net revenue and instructional costs per student, and academic progress as measured by credit accumulation and grade point average, will allow the leaders responsible for enrollment at a given institution to focus on putting resources where they will most contribute to student success and financial sustainability. Being able to view these metrics against benchmarks drawn from comparable institutions speeds the process of identifying areas where an institution is not performing as well as can be expected, and where additional attention seems likely to result in improved performance. Using benchmark comparison groups that include a range of institutions both similar and dissimilar to one's own can still suggest areas where local results can be improved, but using such benchmarks requires more careful interpretation. For this reason, carefully pulling data on an identified peer set from IPEDS or participating in consortium data-sharing efforts where custom peer set reports are available can often be worth the additional cost and labor involved.

However, when pulling select peer data for comparison, it is important to consider the consistency of data definitions across institutions. Where standards such as IPEDS definitions are clear (defining a first-time degree-seeking undergraduate cohort, for example) and your institution can easily submit accurate data, it is reasonable to assume that other institutions do so as well. Where definitions are under local control (such as what constitutes satisfactory academic progress), it is helpful to inquire at other institutions about how they defined their submitted data before interpreting your performance against the benchmark. As with most things in the world of institutional research, there is an unavoidable trade-off between level-of-effort and precision, and how far to go in vetting benchmarks needs to be evaluated against the potential impact of the benchmark for improving institutional performance.

What's Not Available for Comparison with Comparable Institutions?

Sometimes there are no reasonable external benchmark data available. In such cases, the metrics may still be usefully evaluated against internal reference groups. There are two types of internal reference groups to consider: subpopulations and historical performance.

An example of subpopulation benchmarking involves comparing the conversion rate of different prospecting efforts. In this case, it may be more useful to know that prospects purchased from a national testing organization using particular search criteria produced higher conversion rates than prospects purchased from an online college search site, or that mailing a postcard followed by an e-mail produced a conversion rate of 5 percent, while e-mail alone produced only a 4 percent conversion.

Other key metrics where internal comparisons are an important type of benchmark include yields of admitted applicants by various demographic, financial aid, and academic characteristics. Knowing how the yield of in-state students compares to yield of out-of-state students is informative. Knowing how yield differs by the intersection of institutional grant amount and level of demonstrated need can help in developing an awarding strategy. Seeing how retention and graduation rates vary by academic profile information can inform admissions decisions.

Historical comparisons are also important in order to keep strategies current with changing circumstances. In recent years, undergraduate yields have generally been going down as students respond to uncertainty by applying to a larger number of colleges. Plotting the yield trend line for your institution will help you adjust your expectations for the upcoming admissions cycle.

NEW DIRECTIONS FOR INSTITUTIONAL RESEARCH • DOI: 10.1002/ir

Of course, you can combine external, subpopulation, and historical benchmarking approaches. If you have a yield trend line plotted for your institution overall, it would be informative to see how that trend line might differ for in-state and out-of-state applicants. You can also find national yield trend-line data from sources like Noel-Levitz that, while not controlling for institutional characteristics the way a selected peer set would, can at least show how typical your changes in yield are compared to other institutions.

Conclusion

Enrollment management is a complex activity that entails recruiting new students into quality programs with reason to expect they will successfully complete these programs. In order to accomplish these objectives, institutions need to make strategic use of scarce resources. The use of appropriate benchmarks can help an institution identify areas of enrollment management where they are underperforming. Focusing on these areas of unexpectedly low performance can guide institutions on the path toward improved enrollment and student success. These benchmarks do not replace rich institutional and contextual knowledge, but they help enrollment management leaders focus their attention on critical issues.

Note

1. Using IPEDS data tools is beyond the scope of this article. Fortunately, excellent resources are available on the AIR website, www.airweb.org/EducationAndEvents/ IPEDSTraining/Pages/default.aspx

References

Baum, S., and Schwartz, S. "Merit Aid to College Students." *Economics of Education Review*, 1988, 7(1), 127–134.

Bontrager, B. "Enrollment Management: An Introduction to Concepts and Structures." *College and University*, 2004, 79(3), 11–16.

Hossler, D., and others. *The Strategic Management of College Enrollments*. San Francisco: Jossey-Bass, 1990.

Pryor, J. H., Hurtado, S., Saenz, V. B., Korn, W. S. *The American Freshman: Forty Year Trends*. Los Angeles: Higher Education Research Institute, UCLA, 2007.

Voltaire, F.-M. *Dictionnaire Philosophique*. Geneva, Switzerland: Gabriel Grasset, 1764.

Ward, J. "Enrollment Management: Key Elements for Building and Implementing an Enrollment Plan." *College and University*, 2005, 80(4), 7–12.

ROBERT L. DUNIWAY *is an Assistant Vice President for Planning at Seattle University.*

4

This chapter discusses the use of survey data to determine institutions for competitive benchmarking purposes.

Using Institutional Survey Data to Jump-Start Your Benchmarking Process

Timothy K. C. Chow

An unexamined life is not worth living.

—Plato

Self-assessment is a valuable process, not only for individuals but also for organizations, to offer insights into oneself while enhancing understanding of others. All accredited higher education institutions are encouraged by their respective accrediting bodies to take advantage of such a process to identify opportunities for improving performance and striving toward the missions and visions of those institutions. An equally important process known to many institutions, going hand in hand with the self-assessment process, is benchmarking.

Guided by the missions and visions, higher education institutions utilize benchmarking processes to identify better and more efficient ways to carry out their operations. Aside from the initial planning and organization steps involved in benchmarking, a matching or selection step is crucial for identifying other institutions that have good reputations and the best records in the areas of interest for making comparisons. Prior to planning site visits and other in-depth studies, comparative institutional survey data offer a cost-effective way to guide the selection step for locating prospective institutions for benchmarking. A variety of national groups such as the American Association of University Professors (AAUP), American Society for Engineering Education (ASEE), Council for Aid to

NEW DIRECTIONS FOR INSTITUTIONAL RESEARCH, no. 156, Winter 2012 © Wiley Periodicals, Inc.
Published online in Wiley Online Library (wileyonlinelibrary.com) • DOI: 10.1002/ir.20029

Education (CAE), College and University Professional Association for Human Resources (CUPA-HR), Institute of Education Sciences (IES)/ National Center for Education Statistics (NCES), National Association of Colleges and Employers (NACE), National Association of College and University Business Officers (NACUBO), National Science Foundation (NSF), and others, conduct annual institutional surveys on topics such as faculty composition and compensation, financial investment performance and asset allocation, philanthropic support of education, research facilities, student enrollment, financial services, student success, and others. This chapter will provide an overview of how commonly used institutional survey data may jump-start the matching or selection step of the benchmarking process, a discussion of caveats in handling of institutional survey data for comparing baseline data and measuring performance gaps with other institutions, and will offer some suggestions for addressing topic coverage issues associated with using institutional survey data for benchmarking.

Defining Benchmarking

Robert Camp (1989), one of the pioneers in the field of benchmarking, offered a formal definition of benchmarking in the manufacturing context in his text. He quoted David Kearns, a former Xerox Corporation chief executive officer, and defined benchmarking as "the continuous process of measuring products, services, and practices against the toughest competitors or those companies recognized as industry leaders." Camp further provided a more comprehensive working definition for benchmarking as "the search for industry best practices that lead to superior performance." These two definitions align with our operational definition of benchmarking in this volume, where benchmarking is a strategic and structured approach whereby an organization compares aspects of its processes and/ or outcomes to those of another organization or set of organizations in order to identify opportunities for improvement. The emphasis is on continuous and structured process and measurement, with the aim of identifying areas for making improvements.

Approaches or Types of Benchmarking. Ranging from a self-assessment process to a strategic planning process, benchmarking is crucial for examining the effectiveness of current practices, as well as identifying key strategic areas and setting objectives for the strategic goals (Dew and Nearing, 2004). Among the four approaches or types of benchmarking identified by Camp are internal, competitive, functional, and generic. Alstete (1995) noted that the selection of the benchmarking type depends on the processes being analyzed, the availability of data, and the available expertise at the institution. Internal benchmarking involves comparisons of similar operations occurring in different units within an institution, while competitive benchmarking examines process performance among peer

NEW DIRECTIONS FOR INSTITUTIONAL RESEARCH • DOI: 10.1002/ir

institutions in direct competition. Sharron Ronco, in Chapter 2 of this volume, introduces the topic of internal benchmarking and presents the pros and cons of conducting intra-institutional comparison. Functional benchmarking focuses on comparisons of similar operations against leading institutions. With the broadest scope for investigation, generic benchmarking aims at seeking out the best of the best processes for adaptation.

Phases of Benchmarking. The generic phases involved in benchmarking, according to Camp, consist of planning, analysis, integration, action, and maturity. The planning phase involves stating the objectives for the selected type of benchmarking process, determining what and to whom the comparisons should be made, and considering how the data will be collected and interpreted. Following the planning phase, the analysis phase consists of steps to be taken in organizing available information and identifying performance gaps. Next, the integration phase involves communicating the findings, seeking support from key stakeholders, and setting the stage for actions. As the benchmark findings are incorporated into a plan for change, the action phase includes monitoring progress made toward achieving the action plan goals and sharing feedback to all involved in the implementation of the plan. The maturity phase refers to the final stage of the benchmarking process where benchmarking itself becomes a part of the institutional culture for organizational learning and continuous improvement.

Relationships between Self-Assessment and Benchmarking

In these changing times for higher education, it will be advantageous for higher education institutions to conduct routine self-assessment, not just for fulfilling the requirements for accreditation but also for discovering opportunities for making needed improvements with available but increasingly scarce resources. The self-assessment process involves a close examination of one's own performance strengths and weaknesses. After gathering operational data from different units across the institution, the evaluation or sense-making step is crucial to the self-assessment process. Benchmarking can play a role in offering critical input into the evaluation step of the self-assessment process regarding the current performance of one's institution and providing the frame of reference for measuring quality and/or cost of current operations. Considering Alstete's suggested criteria for choosing an approach for benchmarking, often the availability of data can be a hurdle for initiating such a process, particularly when making comparisons beyond one's institution. One way to address this issue is using relevant institutional survey data for supporting the benchmarking effort.

Institutional Researchers' Role in Benchmarking

External reporting is one of the core and common functions performed by institutional research professionals across all types of higher education institutions. Aside from the exposure to a variety of institutional surveys and their corresponding sets of definitions on data elements of various topics, institutional research professionals are often involved in the compilation and upkeep of trend data and key performance indicators for their institutions. Thus, institutional research professionals are more likely to be in a position to lend support to the benchmarking process. As the leadership team of an institution decides on the key activities and performances to be monitored in light of the mission and vision and sets the direction during the planning or organization phase of the benchmarking process, institutional research professionals can contribute to the matching or selection step by gathering relevant background data on other institutions. The source of background data may come from institutional surveys that help identify potential peers or best performers on chosen activities and key processes prior to the more in-depth analysis of performances at the targeted institutions.

Relevant Institutional Survey Data for Benchmarking

Institutional surveys are conducted by a variety of local, regional, state, national, and international groups and organizations. Among them, the Integrated Postsecondary Education Data System (IPEDS) data collection is probably the most familiar one to institutional research professionals in the United States, given its statutory requirement on higher education institutions involved in the federal student financial aid programs. According to the IES and NCES ("About IPEDS," 2012), more than 7,500 institutions complete IPEDS surveys annually on institutional characteristics, enrollments, program completions, graduation rates, faculty and staff, finances, institutional prices, and student financial aid. In Chapter 6 of this volume, Sarah Carrigan offers a detailed discussion on using IPEDS data for supporting peer institution analysis.

Other institutional surveys that are common to higher education institutions may include the Faculty Salary Survey conducted by AAUP; the Voluntary Support of Education (VSE) Survey managed by CAE; the variety of salary, compensation, and benefits programs surveys conducted by CUPA-HR; the Student Survey administered by NACE; the Endowment Study and Tuition Discounting Study conducted by NACUBO; and the Survey of Science and Engineering Research Facilities conducted by NSF. These surveys are designed to capture annual changes on a variety of topics such as faculty composition and compensation, philanthropic support of education, administrative compensation, faculty salaries by disciplinary areas, expectations/plans/activities and starting salaries of college graduates, college investment performance, asset allocation, tuition discount rates and institutional grant aids, and status of research facilities. Aside from gathering data on administrative and operational topics, other higher education groups and research organizations are using institutional surveys to capture information on educational practices associated with student learning. The ones familiar to institutional research professionals may include the National Survey of Student Engagement (NSSE) and its variants administered by the Center for Postsecondary Research (CPR), and the Cooperative Institutional Research Project (CIRP) and related follow-up surveys conducted by the Higher Education Research Institute (HERI). Depending on the priorities and interest areas established during the planning or organization phase of the benchmarking process, institutional survey data may offer insights into the peer or best performer selection step of the process.

Topics to be Addressed by Using Institutional Survey Data

With a focus on a strategic and structured approach, the benchmarking process should begin by addressing the key strategic and relevant issues on achieving the missions and visions of the higher education institutions. A broad range of topics can be explored by utilizing data collected through the institutional surveys mentioned above as an initial step.

Recruitment of Faculty and Staff. For instance, the recruitment and retention of highly qualified faculty and staff can be seen as one of the common strategic goals among higher education institutions. To explore issues related to recruiting and retaining faculty, institutions can utilize AAUP's Faculty Salary Survey data to examine and compare faculty composition and compensation to other institutions in the same region, affiliation, or institutional category. In addition, faculty retention information may be gleaned from the AAUP data for estimating the continuation/turnover rates of faculty. Likewise, CUPA-HR's salary, compensation, and benefits programs surveys may inform decisions among human resources professionals in establishing competitive targets for compensating both faculty and staff in higher education institutions.

Examining Educational Environment and Outcomes. Another common strategic goal often seen among higher education institutions is providing an excellent environment for learning. Research-focused institutions may examine research and development expenditures and other research facilities data collected through the Survey of Research and Development Expenditures at Universities and Colleges and the Survey of Science and Engineering Research Facilities by NSF to detect trends in research and development expenditures by different fields and funding sources. To gain better understanding of characteristics of incoming first-year students and plan for initiatives to engage students in their learning process, institutions may use data from the Cooperative Institutional Research Program (CIRP) Freshman Survey and other related survey data from HERI to detect any differences in the characteristics of incoming students and subsequent developmental changes as students going through the learning process. However, the NSSE and other related survey data

NEW DIRECTIONS FOR INSTITUTIONAL RESEARCH • DOI: 10.1002/ir

collected through the Center for Postsecondary Research (CPR) can be used to examine the educational environment and practices as reported by students within and across participating higher education institutions. Aside from examining students' learning experience during their college years, NACE's Student Survey offers data and insights into job placement outcome, such as student expectations, plans, and activities upon graduation.

Evaluation of Fundraising and Investment Performance. Ensuring that adequate resources are available to support the missions and visions of higher education institutions is of strategic importance. For initiating a review of philanthropic operations, CAE's Voluntary Support of Education (VSE) Survey offers fundraising results, such as sources, purposes, and sizes of charitable gifts and annual alumni giving rate for supporting institutions' self-assessment and benchmarking efforts. To evaluate the performance of endowment, asset allocations, and endowment spending rates, the NACUBO Endowment Study (NES) serves as one of the primary data sources for higher education institutions to examine and adjust their endowment investment and spending policies. These are just a subset of a large collection of postsecondary-related institutional surveys that offer higher education institutions relevant data on topics of interest to assess self-performance or identify other institutions that share similar characteristics on the chosen criteria.

Example of Using Institutional Survey Data for Benchmarking

The following example illustrates how institutional survey data may contribute to the selection step of the benchmarking process. Say a private Midwest technological college has established diversity goals as part of its key strategic initiatives. The college is interested in knowing where it stands in terms of the representation of race and ethnic diversity in the student body. In addition, the college is interested in identifying similar institutions excelling in recruiting and retaining students with diverse racial and ethnic background. It plans to conduct a more in-depth study of approaches and processes at targeted institutions to reveal opportunities for improving student racial and ethnic diversity on campus. By examining the current gaps in maintaining a diverse student body and identifying best practices in addressing the enrollment gaps, the college hopes to realize some of the goals for diversity in instilling abilities to students to interact with people of diverse backgrounds and viewpoints and helping students become global leaders.

Selecting Similar Institutions. In order to learn about the current student mix in terms of race and ethnicity, internal data sources such as a student information system or data warehouse can be utilized to provide the distributions of students by their respective race and ethnic groups. Given the interest in knowing the current standing of student diversity among similar institutions, institutional survey data on fall enrollment, such as IPEDS Fall Enrollment Survey, offers the standardized institutional enrollment data for making initial comparisons across institutions. The criteria for selecting similar institutions can be based on decisions from the college administration, institutional characteristics, existing relationships with other institutions, or published classification categories for higher education institutions. The commonly considered criteria for selecting similar institutions include variables that are collected annually via the IPEDS Institutional Characteristics Header (IC Header) survey, such as governance structure, control, levels, and so on. Other potentially useful criteria such as enrollment mix, program mix, retention and graduation rates, full-time equivalent (FTE) students, and value of endowment assets are also available through the IPEDS data collection. Depending on the chosen criteria, various methods can be applied to evaluate the similarities among institutions such as using cluster analysis to detect homogeneous groups according to the given selection criteria.

Considering input from the college administration and reviewing practices at other higher education institutions, the initial set of selection criteria includes four-year private not-for-profit institutions, Title IV postsecondary institutions, institutions with no religious affiliation, institutions that offer technological degree programs at bachelor's and master's levels, institutions with comparable ranges of SAT scores, and institutions that offered residential facilities to students in city settings. Although data on some of the selection criteria are available via other institutional surveys like the Common Data Set and the guidebook surveys, IES and NCES offer a variety of options and convenient ways to access these data on both individual and a group of institutions online. For identifying similar institutions using institutional survey data already collected through the IPEDS data collection, the online tools provided by IES and NCES should be among the first places to look for available data for comparative analysis.

The preliminary results of identifying similar institutions often require further refinement in subsequent steps to narrow down to a more manageable number of institutions for making comparisons. Additional institutional survey data, such as the Survey of Engineering Colleges by ASEE, may be used in this example to select institutions that share similar instructional focus and program offerings. Once similar institutions are selected and desired performance attributes are identified such as persistence and graduation rates by race and ethnic groups, comparative analysis can be performed to check the current standing of the college on these measures, as well as to identify best performers among similar institutions.

Identifying Best Performers. Considering Camp's working definition for benchmarking mentioned earlier, "the search for industry best practices" is a critical part of the benchmarking process. Traditionally, a "super" index will be derived using average rankings of multiple performance criteria to determine standings among institutions (Laise, 2004). In this case, the "best performer" is the institution receiving the highest averaged value among the rankings of all of the chosen performance criteria. The averaging methodology in general is a reliable data reduction process to allow decision makers to rank institutions according to their average rankings. However, when the rankings of the performance criteria varied significantly for each institution, the average rankings may lead to misleading results. Alternatively, multiple-criteria decision making (MCDM) or multiple-criteria decision analysis (MCDA), such as the multicriteria outranking/ELECTRE methodology proposed by Bernard Roy and his colleagues and discussed by Laise (2004), can be employed to examine if best performers can be chosen among the selected institutions. As the best-performing institutions are selected, direct contact with selected institutions and in-depth interviews and visits can be arranged to study existing approaches and processes implemented at these institutions. The college can utilize this information to confirm performance gaps and to determine appropriate actions to be carried out to make improvements on enhancing student race and ethnic diversity on campus.

Other Opportunities for Data Access. In addition to institutional survey data, higher education institutions may tap into other data resources such as higher education groups, data exchange groups, or consortia to facilitate the comparative analysis process. Some of these resource groups, such as the Carnegie Foundation for the Advancement of Teaching, Higher Education Data Sharing (HEDS) consortium, the Association of American Universities Data Exchange (AAUDE), Southern Universities Group (SUG), and the Consortium for Student Retention Data Exchange (CSRDE) are also using relevant institutional survey data for defining data elements used in the data exchange or deriving performance indicators for supporting self-assessment and benchmarking efforts.

Known Limitations and Issues

Even though institutional surveys cover a wide variety of topics that can be used by higher education institutions for examining performances on the chosen areas or identifying institutions that share similar characteristics using the same measures, there are known limitations associated with institutional survey data for conducting comparative analysis. First and foremost, institutional surveys by nature capture data at the institutional level, while comparisons at times may be required at the programmatic or disciplinary level (Gater, 2003). Second, time lag between the collection and publication of data may present a challenge in allowing for timely analysis of performances and informing subsequent improvement efforts. Moreover, some activities to be examined may require multiple measurements during a given year; however, institutional surveys may only be administered annually due to cost and other factors. Furthermore, changes to the underlying definitions and design of institutional surveys may render the survey data improper for future trend analysis. Finally, some of the institutional surveys may carry vague guidelines or data definitions that will hamper the utility of the survey results for comparative analysis (Teeter and Brinkman, 2003).

Concluding Remarks

Aside from gaining a thorough understanding of the design of the institutional surveys and the quality of the derived data, institutional research professionals may consider applying triangulation techniques by using multiple data sources to verify the authenticity and trustworthiness of the institutional survey data. In addition, more timely and detailed information may be obtained through the participation of data exchange groups or consortia, particularly when the timeliness and breadth of the data for comparative analysis are critical. Last but not least, the benchmarking process is both art and science. Though numerical analysis can offer a more systematic and structural way in assisting the choice-making process, the criteria and threshold selection process often involves subjective decisions and interpretations of preferences and importance of the given criteria. Ultimately, benchmarking is a process that has been shown to promote organizational learning by offering ways to evaluate performance gaps and identify potential improvement opportunities. Utilizing institutional survey data that is already readily available may offer relevant insights into the self-assessment and benchmarking processes, while minimizing resistance and hurdles of doing extra work under the current climate in higher education.

References

"About IPEDS." Integrated Postsecondary Education Data System. Retrieved May 14, 2012, from http://nces.ed.gov/ipeds/about/.

Alstete, J. W. "Benchmarking in Higher Education: Adapting Best Practices to Improve Quality." *ASHE-ERIC Higher Education Report No. 5.* Washington, D.C.: ERIC Digest, 1995.

Camp, R. *Benchmarking: The Search for Industry Best Practices That Lead to Superior Performance.* Milwaukee, Wisc.: ASQC Quality Press, 1989.

Dew, J. R., and Nearing, M. M. *Continuous Quality Improvement in Higher Education.* Westport, Conn.: Praeger, 2004.

Gater, D. S. "Using National Data in University Rankings and Comparisons." Center for Measuring University Performance, 2003.

Laise, D. "Benchmarking and Learning Organizations: Ranking Methods to Identify 'Best in Class.'" *Benchmarking,* 2004, *11*(6), 621–630.

Teeter, D. J., and Brinkman, P. T. "Peer Institutions." In W. Knight (ed.), *The Primer for Institutional Research.* Tallahassee, Fla.: Association for Institutional Research, 2003.

TIMOTHY K. C. CHOW *is the Director of Institutional Research at Rose-Hulman Institute of Technology.*

NEW DIRECTIONS FOR INSTITUTIONAL RESEARCH • DOI: 10.1002/ir

5

This chapter provides a brief overview of baseball sabermetric thinking and demonstrates a simple application of sabermetric methods to benchmarking in a higher education context.

Learning How to Play Ball: Applying Sabermetric Thinking to Benchmarking in Higher Education

Gary D. Levy

Although the notion is certainly clichéd, baseball often serves as an excellent metaphor for life. That said, it is now fair game (no pun intended) to suggest that baseball, and some of the methodologies currently being used to measure, evaluate, manage, and even play it, may serve as references for ways that higher education may be measured, evaluated, managed, and, yes, even played. The present chapter proposes and presents applications of sabermetric thinking and some baseball sabermetric methodologies (James, 1982, 2001; Thorn and Palmer, 1985, 1991) to higher education benchmarking. As such, this chapter aims to offer new tools and thinking for conducting varied higher education benchmarking analyses more judiciously.

There is a reason that mathematicians and statisticians, be they in academia or in more applied or business settings, have an affinity for baseball. Although baseball has qualitative, romantic, and aesthetic aspects (viz. *Field of Dreams;* Kinsella, 1999), it is also a "bean counters" paradise. Quantitative measurement and analysis have been a large part of baseball since its early days when Henry Chadwick created the first rudimentary box score around 1845 (Schiff, 2008), and the Elias brothers first printed baseball scorecards to fans and sold lists of players' batting averages to newspapers in the early 1900s (Schwarz, 2004). Similarly, the arrivals of

NEW DIRECTIONS FOR INSTITUTIONAL RESEARCH, no. 156, Winter 2012 © Wiley Periodicals, Inc.
Published online in Wiley Online Library (wileyonlinelibrary.com) • DOI: 10.1002/ir.20030

institutional research in American higher education, the "quality movement" in American industry (see Chapter 1 of this volume), the assessment movement in higher education, and the call for greater accountability in higher education have combined to give rise to a measurement-minded approach in American higher education. In short, higher education, like baseball, is a "highly competitive and highly measurable activity" (Adler, 2006; Albert and Bennett, 2003).

What Is Sabermetrics?

Sabermetrics is commonly defined as "the search for objective knowledge about baseball" (Grabiner, 1994), although a similar, more common description of sabermetrics as "the mathematical and statistical analysis of baseball" may be more appropriate in the present context (Costa, Huber, and Saccoman, 2008; James, 2001). The "saber" in sabermetrics is derived from the organization termed SABR, or the Society for American Baseball Research. Founded in 1971 by a small group of baseball researchers, SABR's membership now tops 6,000 and is an international enterprise with a large, well-attended, and quantitatively rich annual conference as well as the peer-reviewed *Baseball Research Journal* (now in its forty-first volume) and a large archive of relevant baseball data and publications (www.sabr. org). As noted on the SABR homepage (credited to the late baseball sportscaster Ernie Harwell), "SABR is the Phi Beta Kappa of baseball, providing scholarship which the sport has long needed" (www.sabr.org/about).

One needs only to read the list provided by Costa, Huber, and Saccoman (2009) titled "How to Reason Sabermetrically" to appreciate parallels between sabermetrics and benchmarking in higher education (and for that matter, institutional research).

1. Carefully identify the question(s) under consideration.
2. Get as much relevant data as possible.
3. Use as many measures and instruments as possible.
4. Exercise care with respect to comparisons: try not to compare apples with oranges (make use of the notions of relativity and normalizing when making comparisons).
5. Be conscious of the validity and appropriateness of how things are predicted and how they are measured.
6. Look to see if results from various approaches converge into a plausible solution.
7. Bring into the discussion relevant [qualitative] non-sabermetrical factors (such as history).
8. Be aware of the possibility of further sabermetrical analysis and the development of new tools and measures.
9. Realize that a sabermetrical "proof" is not the same as a mathematical proof.

Institutional researchers involved in higher education benchmarking endeavors abide by many of the same sabermetric principles espoused by Costa, Huber, and Saccoman (2008, 2009). However, there are other, even more apparent parallels between baseball's sabermetric approaches, institutional research, and benchmarking in higher education. Specifically, sabermetrics emerged in baseball for reasons comparable to those that have led to the use of benchmarking in higher education, namely a paradigmatic shift from using "traditional" intuitive and inward-looking approaches to assessing performance using more rigorous analytic and quantitative methods (Lewis, 2003).

Hence, sabermetric approaches may help higher education institutions understand which one(s) of their units, functions, or even personnel are performing well relative to one another (that is, internal benchmarking). For instance perhaps a provost has limited resources and wonders which college(s) should receive those resources based on some type of performance. That is, the provost must ask, "Which is the better/best college in the university in terms of variable X?" Similarly, perhaps a dean has two faculty members with external job offers, but the dean can retain only one of these two. Based on performance, whom should the dean try to retain? Scenarios such as these are common discussions among baseball fans, sabermetricians, and Major League general managers who try to address questions like "which team was really the best in 1995 regardless of which team won the World Series?" or "which of our free-agent players should I try to retain for next year, to the detriment of losing others?"

Similar to Major League baseball teams, higher education institutions (or units within an institution) vie for resources against one another in trying to excel at what they do, and with no distinct rules of fair competition. Moreover, higher education institutions must manage resources creatively and successfully in trying to remain competitive while "competing" against schools that have greater financial resources and are located in superior areas or markets. In these ways, many higher education institutions (or units within institutions) are like small-market baseball teams who must compete against teams in larger markets and with seemingly endless resources (Bradbury, 2007; Lewis, 2003). Therefore, it seems reasonable that higher education institutions could apply sabermetric approaches to be competitive and to put as good a team on the field as their resources could afford (Bradbury, 2007; Schwarz, 2004).

Some Common Sabermetrics

Commonly used baseball "statistics" abound (Albert, 2003; Albert and Bennett, 2003; James, 2001; Thorn and Palmer, 1985, 1991). At the most basic level are *simple counts* of certain activities or products, such as the number of times a batter got to bat (an "at-bat" [AB]), the number of runs a player scores (R), the number of runs a batter bats in (RBI), the number

Table 5.1. Example of a Basic Baseball One-Game Box Score

Player (Batter)	AB	R	H	RBI	BB	SO	LOB	BA
Speaker, CF	5	1	2	0	0	0	1	.400
Chapman, 2B	3	0	1	0	2	1	1	.333
Colavito, RF	4	1	1	1	1	0	6	.250
Boudreau, SS	3	1	1	0	0	0	2	.333
Lajoie, DH	4	0	1	1	0	0	3	.250
Trosky, 1B	4	0	1	1	0	0	0	.250

of hits a batter got (H), or how many walks a batter got (BB). The simple counts methodology is perhaps best exemplified as the basic baseball box score (see Table 5.1); although any sabermetric calculations would be performed on a player's batting data for an entire season and not simply in one game.

Slightly more advanced sabermetric methods combine single-count metrics and use them in calculations of *quotients* or *ratios*. Examples of such quotients or ratios include (for batters) *batting average* (equal to the number of hits a batter got divided by the total number of at-bats the batter had), and *on-base average* (equal to the sum of the number of hits a batter got, plus the number of walks a batter got, plus the number of times a batter was hit by a pitch and awarded first base, divided by the sum of the number of times a batter got an at-bat, plus the number of walks a batter got, plus the number of times a batter was hit by a pitch and awarded first base).[1]

Other, more complex sabermetrics involve *weighted sums*, which include *total bases* (equal to the number of singles multiplied by 1, plus the number of doubles multiplied by the number 2, plus the number of triples multiplied by the number 3, plus the number of home runs multiplied by the number 4).[2] Additional sabermetrics are calculated using a combination of some of the above metrics. Examples include *slugging average* (equal to a hitter's *total bases* divided by total number of at-bats), which is taken as a measure of a hitter's batting power and efficiency in facilitating or scoring runs.

A quick examination of the sabermetrics described so far leads to the following observations: There appears to be a significant amount of sabermetric focus on getting on base, and the number of hits and runs a batter produces. Why this emphasis on getting on base and on hits and scoring runs, one might ask? The answer lies at the heart of how to play baseball or, more specifically, how to win at baseball. Simply put, the baseball team that scores more runs wins the ball game, and the fundamental goal in professional baseball is to win. This truth is borne in the baseball adage "Players are not paid to *play* baseball games. Players are paid to *win* baseball games."

Table 5.2. Some Basic Baseball and Sabermetric Formulae

Statistic	Formula
Batting average (BA)	# hits / # at-bats
On-base average (OBA)	(# hits + # bases on balls + # hit by pitch) / (# at-bats + # bases on balls + # hit by pitch)
Total bases (TB)	((1 * # singles) + (2 * # doubles) + (3 * # triples) + (4 * # home runs))
Slugging average (SA)	# total bases / # at-bats
Runs created (RC)	((# of hits a player got + # of bases on balls a player got) * (TB) / (# of at-bats a player got + # of bases on balls a player got))
Park factor (PF)	((# runs scored at ballpark J + # runs allowed at ballpark J) / (# games played at ballpark J))/ ((# runs scored at ballpark other than J + # runs allowed at ballpark other than J) / (# games played at ballpark other than J))

Logically, then, the value of baseball players should somehow be correlated with how much they get on base and contribute toward scoring runs, and presumably with winning games. To this end, James (James and Henzler, 2002) developed a sabermetric statistic termed *win shares*, which was an attempt to quantify a single index of how greatly an individual player (via hitting, pitching, and/or fielding) contributes toward the total number of wins a team achieves. A discussion of the full calculation of the win shares statistic is beyond the scope of this chapter (Miller, 2006; Ross, 2004), but fortunately James also came up with a "short form" for calculating win shares (as referenced in Costa, Huber, and Saccoman, 2008, 2009). The first step in estimating a win share is to calculate how many runs a player can be credited with having produced, in this case through the *runs created* formula (see Table 5.2).

Sabermetric methods with even greater potential applicability to benchmarking in higher education include methods that afford comparisons between performances of different players and/or teams while adjusting for factors such as ballpark(s). Baseball is unique from other sports because the shapes, sizes, symmetry, and dimensions of the fields on which it is played differ between teams (Costa, Huber, and Saccoman, 2008, 2009). Although rules specify certain aspects of the field of play, such as how many balls count as a walk, the distance from home plate to the pitching mound, the height of the pitching mound, and the distance from one base to another, much else is left for the home team to configure, such as the distance for home runs, the height of outfield fences, and other nuances sometimes called "ground rules." It is no secret that certain ballparks are more conducive to hitters (or "hitter friendly"), particularly power hitters, whereas others are more "pitcher friendly." Similar observations can be made about higher education. Some institutions are more

NEW DIRECTIONS FOR INSTITUTIONAL RESEARCH • DOI: 10.1002/ir

conducive to grant writing or clinical care, whereas others facilitate instructional activities such as undergraduate or graduate education or continuing education.

Calculation of a *park factor* (PF), in its simplest version, begins with calculating the sum of the total number of runs scored by a team at baseball ballpark J plus the total number of runs allowed at baseball ballpark J divided by the total number of games played at ballpark J divided by the sum of the total number of runs scored at a park other than ballpark J plus the total number of runs allowed at a park other than ballpark J divided by the total number of games played at a park other than ballpark J. The concept is rather straightforward—if more runs are scored and/or allowed on average at one ballpark over another, then that ballpark has a park factor that is more "hitter friendly" or less "pitcher friendly" than the other ballpark (see Costa, Huber, and Saccoman, 2008, for a detailed demonstration).

A Modest Application of Sabermetric Thinking to Higher Education Benchmarking

A first step in applying baseball sabermetrics to higher education benchmarking is to develop an academic box score for players of the game (see Table 5.3); in the current case, these players are faculty. Although the academic box score concept may seem fanciful, the simple counting of certain activities or products is commonplace in higher education (Arreola, 2000). Specifically, a faculty member's typical "annual review" might include such simple counts as standard teaching load (STL), class sections taught (CT), total student credit hours generated (SCH), students advised (SA), peer-refereed publications (RP), non-refereed publications (NRP), contracts and grants submitted (CGS), contracts and grants awarded (CGA), and contract and grant award dollars (CGA$).

It is the "box score" of simple counts of activities or products that faculty and administrators frequently focus on in trying to evaluate an individual faculty member or academic unit. Ironically, similar to baseball, these simple counts are often misleading and too simplistic taken alone. The question emerges, then, whether some baseball sabermetric methodologies might be informative when applied to higher education benchmarking.

The measure of success in baseball is clear—namely, winning baseball games—and winning games is accomplished by scoring runs. If one

Table 5.3. Example of a Basic Academic Box Score for Department A

Name	STL	CT	SCH (UG)	SCH (GR)	SCH	SA	RP	NRP	CGS	CGA	CGA$
Doby	6	5	175	20	195	100	3	1	1	1	$10,000
Rosen	6	4	80	40	120	75	2	0	3	1	$25,000

wishes to integrate higher education benchmarking and baseball saber-metric thinking, then the first matter of business would be determining what is meant by "success" in a given higher education setting. In contrast to baseball, a single-outcome measure defining success in higher education is less manageable. Nevertheless, sabermetric methods may still be germane to higher education benchmarking. In the case of higher education, however, there are several related measures of "success" depending partly on one's domain of interest (for example, financial, productivity, instructional, reputational). In this sense, the definition of success is comparable to identification of a performance indicator or measure in traditional benchmarking.

Recall Table 5.3, where a dean has two faculty members who have received external job offers, but the dean can retain only one faculty member. Further, these two faculty members, identified here as Professor Doby and Professor Rosen, are both in Department "A" and appear in the aforementioned academic box score. How should the dean proceed in determining whom to retain? The dean must first decide what type of "success" is to be used in determining each faculty member's value. Let's assume the dean has decided to use revenue generation as the measure of success on which to base the decision. Thus, the dean appears interested in determining which faculty member, Professor Doby or Professor Rosen, is generating the *most revenue* relative to the other.

A *simple count* approach would be to count the number of activities each faculty member engaged in that led to revenue generation, such as number of classes taught, number of student credits (SCH) generated, and number of contracts and grants awarded. This could be thought of as analogous to the number of times a baseball player got on base, in that getting on base frequently results in scoring runs. Another simple count approach would be to get totals for revenue generated by each faculty member from SCH generation and also from contract and grant awards. This is comparable in baseball to counting the number of runs a batter bats in (RBI) or number of runs a player scores (R).

Ratio or *quotient methodologies* could also be applied. For example, in baseball, batting average is the ratio between a batter's number of hits and number of at-bats. Batting average is essentially a measure of batting efficiency. Similarly, a faculty member's *teaching batting average* would be the ratio between the number of classes taught (analogous to getting on base in baseball) by a faculty member and the standard teaching load (STL) for this type of position (analogous to baseball "at-bats"). Similarly, a faculty member's *contracts and grants batting average* would be the number of contracts and grants awarded to a faculty member divided by the number of contracts and grants submitted by that faculty member. Finally, a faculty member's *academic on-base average* would be the sum of the number of classes taught and the number of grants and contracts awarded divided by the sum of the standard teaching load for this faculty member and

NEW DIRECTIONS FOR INSTITUTIONAL RESEARCH • DOI: 10.1002/ir

Table 5.4. Some Possible Academic Sabermetric Formulae

Statistic	Formula
Teaching batting average (TBA)	# of classes taught / # of classes in standard teaching load
Contracts and grants batting average (CGBA)	# of contracts and grants awarded / # of contracts and grants submitted
Academic on-base average (AOBA)	(# of classes taught plus # of contracts and grants awarded) / (# of classes in standard teaching load plus # of contracts and grants submitted)
Academic revenue total bases (ARTB)	(($300 * # of undergraduate SCH) plus ($700 * # of graduate SCH) plus (contracts and grants awarded $))

Table 5.5. Academic Sabermetrics for Professors Doby and Rosen in Department A

Name	Teaching Batting Average	Contracts and Grants Batting Average	Academic On-Base Average	Academic Revenue Total Bases
Doby	0.833	1.000	0.857	$76,500
Rosen	0.667	0.333	0.556	$77,000

the number of grants and contracts the faculty member submitted (see Table 5.4).

The aforementioned simple counts and ratio methodologies provide simple descriptions of the efficiency and productivity for each faculty member in terms of activities that have the potential to generate revenue. However, the dean is also interested in determining which faculty member, Professor Doby versus Professor Rosen, is generating the *most revenue* for the institution relative to the other. In this particular instance undergraduate SCH generate $300 per SCH, whereas graduate SCH produce $700 per SCH. Hence, at the simplest level, the dean can see that Professor Doby generated total SCH revenue of *$66,500* ($52,500 undergraduate plus $14,000 graduate), whereas Professor Rosen generated *$52,000* ($24,000 undergraduate plus $28,000 graduate).

Adding academic revenue generated by contract and grant awards to these results in a formula comparable to a baseball batter's *total bases (TB)*, namely ((SCH1 * $300) + (SCH2 * $700) + ($ from contracts and grants awarded)). Using this formula, Professor Rosen moves slightly ahead of Professor Doby by *$77,000* to *$76,500* (see Table 5.5).

Based on this, it might make sense for the dean to conclude that Professor Rosen should be retained over Professor Doby. That is, in this instance, Professor Rosen appears to have generated more total revenue than Professor Doby, and this is presumably what interests the dean most. But let's challenge this conclusion by developing an analog to the baseball batter *slugging average* for Professors Rosen and Doby.

NEW DIRECTIONS FOR INSTITUTIONAL RESEARCH • DOI: 10.1002/ir

Table 5.6. Some Additional Possible Academic Sabermetric Formulae

IR-Sabermetric Statistic	Formula(e)
Academic revenue **slugging average** (ARSA)	Academic Revenue Total Bases / (# of classes in standard teaching load plus # of contracts and grants submitted)
Academic revenue **runs created** (ARRC)	Academic Revenue Total Bases / (# of classes in standard teaching load plus # of contracts and grants submitted)
Academic Revenue **park factor** (ARPF)	((# of classes taught plus # of contracts and grants awarded) * (Academic Revenue Total Bases)) / (# of classes in standard teaching load plus # of contracts and grants submitted)

In baseball, slugging average is equal to a player's *total bases* divided by that player's number of at-bats. That is, slugging average takes into consideration both a player's batting efficiency (*batting average* or how often the player got a hit relative to number of opportunities to get a hit) as well as the player's power (*total bases* or how many bases [or potential runs] a player got when the player in fact got on base). For example, imagine there were two batters and each achieved getting on base (hitting a single, hitting a double, hitting a triple, getting walked, or getting hit by a pitch). Would the value of each of these two batters (value being defined as the likelihood of scoring runs) be the same? Clearly not. The value of the batter in this case depends on *how* each batter got on base. For example, a triple would be a more valuable hit compared to a single, and a home run would be better than a double or triple. Let's apply similar thinking in comparing academic revenue generation of Professors Rosen and Doby.

Unfortunately, deriving a method for calculating an academic version of slugging average may not be as straightforward as in baseball. But it is still worth examination. The *academic revenue slugging average* for Professor Rosen (see formula in Table 5.6) would be ($77,000 / (6 + 3)) = $12,836, whereas for Professor Doby it is ($76,500 / (6 + 1)) = $12,751. This finding suggests that when Professor Rosen participates in activities that can lead to revenue generation (that is, an academic at-bat), he demonstrates only slightly greater power for revenue generation (analogous to run generation, or slugging average, in baseball) than Professor Doby.

However, now let's extend sabermetric thinking one step further and move beyond use of slugging average. *Academic revenue slugging average* is a neat means to evaluate revenue generation performance, but it does not take into consideration the amount or efficiency of effort each faculty member put into generating his/her academic revenue. In this case, Professor Rosen generates slightly more academic revenue than Professor Doby but does so by (1) teaching *fewer* classes than Professor Doby (which in this instance is considered unfavorable since it essentially

Table 5.7. Additional IR-Sabermetrics for Professors Doby and Rosen in Department

Name	Academic Revenue Total Bases	Academic Revenue Slugging Average	Academic Revenue Runs Created
Doby	$76,500	$12,751	$65,571
Rosen	$77,000	$12,836	$42,778

amounts to a lost opportunity to generate more SCH revenue, akin to not taking advantage of an academic at-bat), and (2) writing and submitting three times *more* contracts and grants to get one awarded than Professor Doby.

The *academic revenue runs created* metric provides a different measure of revenue generation efficiency because it considers efficiency in terms of number of courses taught in relation to standard teaching load, as well as number of contracts and grants awarded in relation to number of contracts and grants submitted (see Table 5.7). Specifically, whereas Professor Rosen generated greater academic revenue total bases, and also demonstrated a better *academic revenue slugging average* than Professor Doby, he did so less efficiently (as evidenced by a lower teaching batting average as well as a lower contracts and grants batting average than Professor Doby). The academic revenue runs created formula takes into consideration these two averages and, in doing so, reveals that Professor Doby demonstrated greater efficiency in generating academic revenue compared to Professor Rosen (and perhaps better continued potential toward revenue generation as well).

The preceding example involving Professors Rosen and Doby works well, in part, because both reside in the same department (or the same "academic ballpark"). However, how would the dean have proceeded if the two faculty members with external offers were from different departments? In a second example scenario, Professor Doby and Professor Joss are from the same college but different departments, both have external offers, but the dean can retain only one. In this instance, the dean could consider applying the sabermetric principle of *park factor* to determine whether one academic department is more academic revenue generation "friendly" than the other.

Tables 5.8 and 5.9 provide some academic sabermetric information for Professors Doby and Professor Joss. At face value Professor Joss appears to outperform Professor Doby across all three measures. However, before making any conclusions, the dean also needs to see more academic sabermetric information for each of the departments in which these two professors reside.

The dean also knows that the two departments housing Professors Doby and Joss have the departmental academic box scores shown in Table

**Table 5.8. Academic Sabermetrics for Professors Doby
(Department A) and Professor Joss (Department B)**

Name	Academic Revenue Total Bases	Academic Revenue Slugging Average	Academic Revenue Runs Created
Doby	$76,500	$12,751	$65,571
Joss	$150,000	$75,254	$75,250

**Table 5.9. Departmental Academic Scorecard for Department A
(Professors Doby) and Department B (Professor Joss)**

Department	STL	CT	SCH (UG)	SCH (GR)	SCH$	CGS	CGA	CGA$
A (Doby's)	72	63	1,555	455	$785,000	11	4	$75,000
B (Joss')	22	18	580	210	$321,000	12	8	$540,000

5.9. Based on these data, Departments A and B generated comparable total academic revenue of *$860,000* ($785,000 + $75,000) and *$861,000* ($321,000 + $540,000), respectively. However, do the data suggest any type of academic ballpark factor in terms of relative ease in generating academic revenue? Calculations of academic ballpark factor for each department provide an academic ballpark factor of 0.41 for Department A, and 2.44 for Department B (see Table 5.6 for the academic ballpark factor formula). These two academic ballpark factors suggest that it is relatively "easier" to engage successfully in activities that result in academic revenue generation in Department B than Department A.

These academic park factor findings dampen the observed difference in academic revenue runs created between Professors Joss and Doby. Specifically, these results suggest that Department B provides greater likelihood for its faculty to engage successfully in activities leading to academic revenue generation compared to what is afforded faculty in Department A. Put another way, Department B is more academic revenue generation "friendly" than Department A. This result likely arises from the higher percentage of graduate SCH relative to overall SCH and a higher contracts and grants batting average in Department B compared to in Department A. These factors, in combination with an advantage in academic revenue slugging average in Department B relative to Department A ($25,323 versus $10,361, respectively) help make Department B an academic ballpark more amenable to academic revenue generation than Department A. Of course, if we compared Department B to another department, for instance, a department in a different college or at a more research-intensive institution, then perhaps the tables would be turned in terms of park factors and academic revenue "friendliness."

In the end, the dean must weigh all of these sabermetric findings and make a decision. The dean would do well to return to the tenets of sabermetric thinking espoused earlier, and consider relevant qualitative information about these two faculty members and departments, as well as thinking critically about validity and appropriateness of these academic sabermetric statistics. Ultimately the dean will probably need to use quantitative and qualitative, and objective and subjective, information as well as judgment and intuition to decide which faculty member to try and retain. Hopefully, the findings weaned using sabermetric methodologies would afford keener and more judicious decision making.

Conclusions

Thinking and decision-making in baseball have evolved from intuition and simple counting and ratio approaches to more sophisticated sabermetric methodologies. The present chapter proposes borrowing from baseball sabermetric thinking and applying its methodologies to situations within higher education. The present examples have focused only on financial information, but this is not to say that sabermetric methodologies can be used only with these types of data. The examples and applications presented in this chapter are less than fully refined and deserve critical examination; however, the singular objective was to "throw out the first pitch" regarding application and integration of sabermetric thinking into higher education benchmarking and to see what comes of it. That said, it is now time to "play ball."

Notes

1. On-base average takes into consideration both at-bats and plate appearance (that is, walks, hit by pitch). It is important for the baseball novice to understand that batters who reach base by being walked or hit by a pitch are *not* credited with an official at-bat.
2. The batting runs statistic (BR, equal to the number of singles multiplied by 0.41, plus the number of doubles multiplied by 0.82, plus the number of triples multiplied by 1.06, plus the number of home runs multiplied by 1.42) is a more refined version of the total bases statistic and one with potential utility in higher education contexts. The batting run sabermetric has many versions but is based largely on multiple regression and linear weights methodologies that assign a coefficient to each variable (in this case, number of singles, doubles, and so on) in predicting the total number of runs scored (Costa and others, 2009; Thorn and Palmer, 1985, 1991).

References

Adler, J. *Baseball Hacks: Tips and Tools for Analyzing and Winning with Statistics.* Sebastopol, Calif.: O'Reilly, 2006.

Albert, J. *Teaching Statistics Using Baseball.* Washington, D.C.: Mathematical Association of America, 2003.

Albert, J., and Bennett, J. *Curve Ball: Baseball, Statistics, and the Role of Chance in the Game.* New York: Copernicus Books, 2003.

Arreola, R. A. *Developing a Comprehensive Faculty Evaluation System.* Boston: Anker, 2000.

Bradbury, J. C. *The Baseball Economist: The Real Game Exposed.* New York: Dutton, 2007.

Costa, G. B., Huber, M. R., and Saccoman, J. T. *Understanding Sabermetrics: An Introduction to the Science of Baseball Statistics.* Jefferson, N.C.: McFarland and Company, 2008.

Costa, G. B., Huber, M. R., and Saccoman, J. T. *Practicing Sabermetrics: Putting the Science of Baseball Statistics to Work.* Jefferson, N.C.: McFarland and Company, 2009.

Grabiner, D. J. "The Sabermetric Manifesto," 1994. Retrieved November, 2012, from neohumanism.org/s/sa/sabermetrics.html.

James, B. *The Bill James Baseball Abstract.* New York: Ballantine, 1982.

James, B. *The New Bill James Historical Baseball Abstract.* New York: Free Press, 2001.

James, B., and Henzler, J. *Win Shares.* Skokie, Ill.: STATS, Inc., 2002.

Kinsella, R. *Shoeless Joe.* New York: Houghton Mifflin, 1999.

Lewis, M. *Moneyball: The Art of Winning an Unfair Game.* New York: Norton, 2003.

Miller, S. J. "A Derivation of the Pythagorean Win-Loss Formula in Baseball," 2006. Retrieved November, 2012, from web.williams.edu/go/math/sjmiller/public_html/math/papers/PythagWonLoss_Paper.pdf.

Ross, K. A. *Mathematician at the Ballpark: Odds and Probabilities for Baseball Fans.* New York: PI Press, 2004.

Schiff, A. J. *The Father of Baseball: A Biography of Henry Chadwick.* Jefferson, N.C.: McFarland and Company, 2008.

Schwarz, A. *The Numbers Game: Baseball's Lifelong Fascination with Statistics.* New York: St. Martin's Press, 2004.

Thorn, J., and Palmer, P. *The Hidden Game of Baseball.* Garden City, N.Y.: Doubleday, 1985.

Thorn, J., and Palmer, P. *Total Baseball.* New York: Warner, 1991.

GARY D. LEVY *is Associate Provost of Academic Resources and Planning and Professor of Psychology at Towson University (as well as an avid baseball fan).*

NEW DIRECTIONS FOR INSTITUTIONAL RESEARCH • DOI: 10.1002/ir

6

This chapter discusses how institutions can use IPEDS data to assist their institution to determine what other institutions should be used in external benchmark analysis.

Selecting Peer Institutions with IPEDS and Other Nationally Available Data

Sarah D. Carrigan

The process of identifying and selecting peers for a college or university is one of this volume's definitions for *benchmarking*: "a strategic and structured approach whereby an organization compares aspects of its processes and/or outcomes to those of another organization or set of organizations to identify opportunities for improvement." The higher education and institutional research literature is rich with descriptions of peer types, purposes, and data sources for peer selection, going back nearly forty years. Curry (1972) appears to be the earliest to describe a need for comparison institutions and a peer selection process. Types of peers (Brinkman and Krakower, 1983; Brinkman and Teeter, 1987; Teeter and Brinkman, 2003) have been defined and refined, along with selection methods and variables (Terenzini, Hartmark, Lorang, and Shirley, 1980; Teeter and Christal, 1987; Brinkman and Teeter, 1987; Ingram, 1995; Prather and Carlson, 1991; Weeks, Puckett, and Daron, 2000; Zhao and Dean, 1997). Hurley (2002) provides an extensive literature review, and Trainer (2008) discusses issues and data sources, and the context of the role of the institutional research profession in peer selection and analysis. Soldner (2009) investigated the use of IPEDS peer data products, among "campus-based practitioners, and how those products might be improved" (p. 4).

As a case study, this chapter will describe empirical data available in several national data sources that can be used to identify potential peers-based criteria important to the institution. These data sources include the

NEW DIRECTIONS FOR INSTITUTIONAL RESEARCH, no. 156, Winter 2012 © Wiley Periodicals, Inc.
Published online in Wiley Online Library (wileyonlinelibrary.com) • DOI: 10.1002/ir.20031

Integrated Postsecondary Education Data System (IPEDS), the NCES Library Statistics program, the College and University Professional Association for Human Resources (CUPA-HR), and the Carnegie Classification of Institutions of Higher Education. Then the chapter will turn to describing the development of a web-based peer selection tool developed by the system office of the University of North Carolina, and will conclude with a description of the peer selection process executed by the University of North Carolina at Greensboro campus (UNCG).

Integrated Postsecondary Education Data System (IPEDS)

IPEDS comprises a data collection cycle focused on U.S. postsecondary education. It operates within the National Center for Education Statistics (NCES), a part of the Institute for Education Sciences within the United States Department of Education. IPEDS consists of nine interrelated survey elements collected each year. The survey cycle is mandatory for all institutions that participate in or are applicants for participation in any federal financial assistance program authorized by Title IV of the Higher Education Act of 1965, as amended. The department was created in 1992 and began collecting data in 1993.

Each year, IPEDS collects data in seven general areas: institutional characteristics, institutional prices, enrollment, student financial aid, degrees and certificates conferred, student persistence and success, and institutional human and fiscal resources. The data are linked to the institutional Unit ID number, an identification system developed by NCES. This rich set of measures is made available to interested users through several web-based data retrieval and report-generation systems, including the IPEDS Data Center (http://nces.ed.gov/ipeds/datacenter/) and the Data Analysis System (http://nces.ed.gov/das/). The IPEDS Data Center allows users to retrieve institutional data for single or multiple institutions. The user can design trend reports, calculate descriptive statistics, compare institutions with group averages, and download data files. The Data Analysis System provides similar access to data collected in a series of education surveys administered periodically to postsecondary students, graduates, and faculty.

Association for Institutional Research and IPEDS

Typically, the institutional research function within a U.S. college or university has responsibility for collecting and submitting these required data to IPEDS. As a part of its professional development function, the Association for Institutional Research (AIR) maintains an IPEDS training and support area within its website (www.airweb.org/EducationAndEvents/IPEDSTraining/Pages/default.aspx). AIR provides online tutorials, workshops, and other online resources that allow the institutional researcher to learn and remain up to date on IPEDS data requirements and data retrieval tools.

Library Statistics Program

NCES began a nationwide library statistics program in 1989, including the Academic Libraries Survey, collected biennially in even-numbered fiscal years from about 3,700 degree-granting postsecondary institutions. Data collected comprise the library's administrative and operational details. These include library staff and salaries/wages, and other library expenditures on information resources and operating expenditures. Library collections are reported, including both the number of new collections added during the reported fiscal year and the total number held at the end of the fiscal year. Library services are another focus area on the Academic Libraries Survey, which includes services such as interlibrary loans, documents delivered from commercial services, electronic services provided by the library, and institutional support for information literacy (support for skills needed to find, retrieve, analyze, and use information).

Similar to the IPEDS Data Center, NCES provides a website that allows users to create reports that compare a library of interest with a comparison group on selected information from the Academic Libraries Survey. In addition, the data files for surveys collected since 1996 are available for download in multiple formats (http://nces.ed.gov/surveys/libraries/aca_data.asp). The data files allow researchers to perform additional data analysis that is not available in the web tool and other publications. Data are organized by institution, including the institutional Unit ID number.

CUPA-HR Surveys and Data on Demand

CUPA-HR is the professional association focused on human resource issues in higher education. CUPA-HR administers a series of compensation and salary surveys each year to U.S. colleges and universities that collect information about faculty, senior administrators, midlevel professionals, and contingent faculty. It publishes benchmarking reports with national mean and median salaries, available for purchase each spring. An additional fee allows users direct access to the survey data for additional analysis, built around comparison groups created by the user. This service is known as *DataOnDemand* (www.cupahr.org/surveys/dod.asp#dod). Unlike the IPEDS Data Center, individual institution data are not identified or made available to the user.

Carnegie Classification of Institutions of Higher Education

The Carnegie Foundation for the Advancement of Teaching (www.carnegiefoundation.org) is an independent policy and research center focused on the improvement of teaching and learning. Within that mission, the foundation has a classification system of colleges and universities that allow operational and benchmark comparisons among similar institutions with the Carnegie system. While the Carnegie Foundation has published its classification system since 1973, it has updated and expanded the focus several times in subsequent years. The current framework, updated in 2010, includes six classifications in which all campuses are categorized. These are the Basic classification, Undergraduate and Graduate Instructional Program classifications, Enrollment Profile and Undergraduate Profile classifications, and the Size and Setting classification. In addition, the Carnegie Foundation introduced an elective classification for Community Engagement in 2006. The Carnegie Foundation (n.d.) specifies:

> Community Engagement describes the collaboration between institutions of higher education and their larger communities (local, regional/state, national, global) for the mutually beneficial exchange of knowledge and resources in a context of partnership and reciprocity.

Institutions may voluntarily participate in this classification and complete an extensive documentation process to demonstrate the campus's level of community engagement. The Carnegie Foundation website allows users to look up institutions, as well as list and download groups of institutions that meet criteria of interest to the user.

UNC System Peer Requirement

Since about the mid-1990s, the University of North Carolina (UNC) has required that each of its constituent postsecondary campuses select a set of peer institutions by which the campus would be compared in operational and outcome areas. The UNC Board of Governors has final authority to approve each campus peer list. The comparisons can include items such as tuition and fees, faculty salaries, faculty workload and teaching load, faculty diversity, endowments, and budget and fiscal measures. Periodically, the campuses are directed to review and update their peer lists. In the spring of 2011, UNC General Administration (UNC-GA) directed each of the constituent campuses to begin a peer review process, in order "to reassess campus peers using more recent national data and consider the economic realities" (B. Mallette, personal communication, May 2011). In preparation for that project, the system office UNC-GA developed a web-based peer selection tool (PST; http://fred.northcarolina.edu/pub/html/peers.html) that allows each access to a large set of IPEDS data for the 2009–10 collection cycle, for the entire set of U.S. institutions that submitted IPEDS data.

UNC-GA provided a number of ground rules to consider while each campus developed its set of potential peers. The target peers for each campus were between thirteen and eighteen public institutions from outside North Carolina in the same Carnegie classification (Basic classification). The primary intent was to establish a list of institutions which each UNC campus regularly compares itself with because of current similarities. However, there is value in identifying aspirational peers: those which the campus seeks to become more like over time. Each UNC campus was allowed to select up to three aspirational peers for their peer set.

The PST was constructed to allow the user to control the weights of variables on which to compare a target institution against other institutions. Seventy comparison variables are loaded into the PST, in general categories of Institutional Characteristics, Student Characteristics, Student Finances, Faculty and Expenses, Revenue Sources, and Degrees Awarded. Table 6.1 lists the specific set of data items available in the PST. The PST includes both categorical and continuous variables. Many of the continuous variables are presented as percentages or ratios, such as six-year graduation rate, percent of minority students, and percent of full-time faculty. Other data are presented as percentile variables, where the institutional values in the IPEDS data set were transformed to percentile scores, each based on the range of reported scores from the approximate 6,000 institutions in the IPEDS universe. The PST uses a weighted distance index that ranks all relevant institutions in comparison to the target institution. Variables can be weighted to allow relative importance of individual variables to be included in calculating the index. The lower the index score, the more that institution resembles the target institution on the selected variables.

UNCG Peer Selection Process. Selecting a set of peer institutions by which a campus will measure and be measured requires a thoughtful, deliberative process involving a variety of institutional stakeholders. At UNCG the primary stakeholders directly involved in the 2011 peer selection were senior academic leadership, including the provost, academic deans, the vice chancellor for research and economic development, and the dean of the library, known as the Deans Council. The director of institutional research initiated and supported the peer discussion and selection process during an approximate five-month project time frame established by UNC-GA. Upon review of the many variables available in PST, it was determined that a much shorter list of criteria would be of interest for UNCG. This set of variables (Table 6.2) quantifies topics and issues that are important to UNCG, such as student success, underserved populations, and academic program mix.

A preliminary list of seventy public campuses in the same Carnegie class as UNCG was prepared and presented to the Deans Council. These institutions were selected based on close individual similarity with UNCG in each of the fourteen criteria. The seventy campuses were rank-ordered based on the number of criteria for which they were similar to UNCG. Following this first review by the Deans Council, the vice chancellor for

Table 6.1. UNC-GA Peer Selection Tool

Institutional Characteristics
Region
Level
Control
Highest degree level
HBCU status
Includes a medical school
Includes a veterinary school
Locale
Carnegie 2005 classification
Carnegie 2000 classification
Land grant institution status
Size category
Student Characteristics
Total head count
Total FTE
FTE-to-head count ratio
Six-year FTE growth rate
Percentage of undergraduate FTE
Percentage of graduate FTE
Percentage minority
Percentage of undergrads over age
twenty-five
Percentage of all students over age
twenty-five
Six- or three-year graduation rate
Five-year graduation rate
Four-year graduation rate
FT frosh-soph retention rate
PT frosh-soph retention rate
Student-to-faculty ratio
Percentage taking SAT
25th percentile SAT
75th percentile SAT
Percentage taking ACT
25th percentile ACT
75th percentile ACT
Freshman selectivity (percentage of
rejected applicants)

Student Finances
Percentage of UG receiving grant aid
Average amount of grant aid
Percentage of UG receiving Pell grants
Average amount of Pell grants
Percentage of UG receiving federal loans
Average amount of federal loans
In-state UG tuition and fees
Out-of-state UG tuition and fees
In-state graduate tuition and fees
Out-of-state graduate tuition and fees
Faculty and Expenses
Total instructional faculty
Percentage of full-time instructional faculty
Average faculty salary
Percentage of expenditures on instruction
Percent of Expenditures on Research
Percentage of expenditures on public service
Revenue Sources
Average tuition per FTE
Average federal revenue per FTE
Average state/local revenue per FTE
Average total revenue per FTE
Percentage of revenue from tuition
Percentage of revenue from federal
Percentage of revenue from state/local
Endowment per FTE
Degrees Awarded
Number of degrees awarded
Degrees per average 100 head count
enrollment
Percentage less than four years
Percentage bachelor's
Percentage master's
Percentage doctor's
Percent in humanities and social sciences
Percentage in education
Percentage in agriculture and STEM
Percentage in business and public
administration
Percentage in communication and art
Percentage in health professions

research and economic development prepared a separate list of Carnegie High and Very High Research institutions, which also have earned the Carnegie classification on Community Engagement. UNCG is a High Research institution. In addition, the dean of the library requested to review library statistics available from the 2008 administration of the IPEDS Library Survey, including:

NEW DIRECTIONS FOR INSTITUTIONAL RESEARCH • DOI: 10.1002/ir

Table 6.2. Peer Selection Criteria Used

Retention rate
Six-year graduation rate
UG Tuition and fees
Degrees awarded
Student headcount
Average faculty salary
Number of instructional faculty
Percent of degrees in education
Percent of degrees in humanities and social sciences
Percent of expenditures on instruction
Percent minority
Percent of UG FTE
Percent of UG receiving grant aid
Percent of UG receiving pell grants

- Holdings: Books, serial backfiles, and other
- Expenditures for books, serial backfiles, and other
- Total expenditures
- Total staff in FTE

The director of institutional research merged and cross-referenced these additional data points to identify campuses that continue to show similarities to UNCG on as many items as possible. Subsequent discussions among members of the Deans Council identified that student head count, graduation rates, retention rates, undergraduate tuition and fees, average faculty salary, community engagement, and library holdings and expenditures would gain specific attention and elevation. Recommendations about specific campuses to consider as direct peers or aspirational campuses were elicited from individual stakeholders. A preliminary list was agreed upon by UNCG stakeholders and submitted to UNC-GA for consideration. Several more rounds of negotiation occurred between UNCG and UNC-GA. A final list of fifteen peers and three aspirational campuses was presented to the UNCG Deans Council and the UNCG chancellor for final consultation in early September. Upon campus leadership approval, the 2011 UNC-approved peers for UNCG were reviewed and approved in fall 2011 by the UNC Board of Governors.

This chapter has described performance data and rational processes available for institutional peer selection. Disparate data sources that use a common institutional identification system can be readily merged to build larger datasets containing a wide variety of data points. Benchmarks or target outcomes can be identified based on the average or peak performance of the peer set. Presumably, similar institutions face similar opportunities and challenges, allowing performance goals that are rational and achievable. A set of carefully selected peer institutions allows a campus to compare its performance in operational areas that the campus values, on a variety of metrics with institutions that are most like it.

References

Brinkman, P. T., and Krakower, J. *Comparative Data for Administrators in Higher Education*. Boulder, Colo.: National Center for Higher Education Management Systems, 1983.

Brinkman, P. T., and Teeter, D. J. "Methods for Selecting Comparison Groups." In P. T. Brinkman (ed.), *Conducting Institutional Comparisons*. New Directions for Institutional Research (no. 53, pp. 5–23). San Francisco: Jossey Bass, 1987.

Carnegie Foundation. "Carnegie Classifications." n.d. Retrieved November 28, 2012, from Carnegie Foundation Web Site: http://classifications.carnegiefoundation.org/descriptions/community_engagement.php.

Curry, D. J. *The Seven Comparison States: Their Selection, Use and Applicability for Higher Education*. Boulder, Colo.: National Center for Higher Education Management Systems, 1972.

Hurley, R. G. "Identification and Assessment of Community College Peer Institution Selection Systems." *Community College Review*, 2002, 29(4), 1–26.

Ingram, J. A. *Using IPEDS for Selecting Peer Institutions*. Lincoln, Nebr.: Coordinating Commission for Postsecondary Education, 1995.

Prather, J. E., and Carlson, C. E. "Using Institutional Comparisons for Administrative Decision Support." (ERIC Document Reproduction Service No. ED335794), 1991.

Soldner, M. "Peer Comparison Data: Meeting The Needs Of Campus Decision-Makers." AIR/NCES Data Policy Fellowship Report, 2009.

Teeter, D. J., and Brinkman, P. T. "Peer Institutions." In W. E. Knight (ed.), *The Primer for Institutional Research*. Tallahassee, Fla.: Association for Institutional Research, 2003.

Teeter, D. J., and Christal, M. E. "Establishing Peer Groups: A Comparison of Methodologies." *Planning for Higher Education*, 1987, 15(2), 8–17.

Terenzini, P. T., Hartmark, L., Lorang, W. G., and Shirley, R. C. "A Conceptual and Methodological Approach to the Identification of Peer Institutions." *Research in Higher Education*, 1980, 12(4), 347–364.

Trainer, J. F. "The Role of Institutional Research in Conducting Comparative Analysis of Peers." In D. G. Terkla (ed.), *Institutional Research: More Than Just Data*. New Directions for Higher Education (no. 141, pp. 21–30). San Francisco: Jossey-Bass, 2008.

Weeks, S. F., Puckett, D., and Daron, R. "Developing Peer Groups for the Oregon University System: From Politics to Analysis (and Back)." *Research in Higher Education*, 2000, 41(1), 1–20.

Zhao, J., and Dean, D. C. "Selecting Peer Institutions: A Hybrid Approach." Paper presented at the Annual Forum of the Association for Institutional Research, Orlando, Fla., 1997.

SARAH D. CARRIGAN is the Director of Institutional Research at the University of North Carolina at Greensboro.

NEW DIRECTIONS FOR INSTITUTIONAL RESEARCH • DOI: 10.1002/ir

7

This chapter researches whether a link exists between public top-tier institutions and their host municipalities. The study then researches whether the same link exists in the state of Texas's "Emerging Universities."

Benchmarking Tier-One Universities: "Keeping Up with the Joneses"

Nicolas A. Valcik, Kimberly E. Scruton, Stuart B. Murchison, Ted J. Benavides, Todd Jordan, Andrea D. Stigdon, Angela M. Olszewski

Over the past decade, the *U.S. News and World Report* (USNWR) "America's Best College" ranking system has shaped higher education policy as institutions across the United States strive to be listed as a top-tier university or college. This ranking system relies on several metrics, including strong metrics like student retention and graduation rates and more arbitrary measures like the peer analysis score, to compare institutions. While there are many critics of USNWR's methodology, there is little doubt that the rankings have inspired many university administrators to adjust their policies to take the USNWR metrics into consideration and strive to produce the best outcomes possible to increase their institutions' rankings. An example of this type of policy "adjustment" was raised by Catherine Watt, the former institutional research director of Clemson University, who stated that class size was reduced by Clemson's administration in order to achieve a higher USNWR ranking (Pope, 2009). This drive to improve rankings can extend into state legislation. In 2009, the state of Texas designated seven of its public universities as "Emerging Universities," thus making them eligible to receive additional funding based on their abilities to boost their USNWR rankings into the top tier.

The impetus behind the Emerging Universities initiative can be traced to President David E. Daniel's effort to obtain legislative support for

NEW DIRECTIONS FOR INSTITUTIONAL RESEARCH, no. 156, Winter 2012 © Wiley Periodicals, Inc.
Published online in Wiley Online Library (wileyonlinelibrary.com) • DOI: 10.1002/ir.20032

boosting the University of Texas at Dallas into the top-tier rankings as a means to acquire more monetary resources for his institution (*Dallas Morning News*, 2009). To accomplish this task, Dr. Daniel wrote an executive summary titled "Thoughts on Creating More Tier One Universities in Texas," which outlined the benefits that more public top-tier institutions could provide to the state of Texas, not the least of which is to stem the tide of Texas's "brain drain" as more high school graduates leave the state to attend college (Daniel, 2008). Dr. Daniel also argued that top-tier research institutions provide economic stimulus through their research efforts by providing jobs and by producing well-educated and well-trained workers for local businesses. The state legislature responded by passing House Bill 51 to fund and support seven Texas public universities in their efforts to obtain top-tier status (Texas Higher Education Coordinating Board, 2009).

The economic impact of a top-tier institution on its host community is often a core argument behind university efforts to achieve higher rankings. Most USNWR metrics rely on student quality, and high-quality students are drawn to universities with prestigious reputations, reputations earned not only by the kind of students admitted but by the research conducted by their faculty. Well-educated graduates from prestigious institutions are desired by businesses seeking highly skilled employees. Universities themselves generate economic development by simply being present: They represent a large population of students and tax-paying employees who eat at local restaurants, shop at local stores, and live in local housing. The State University of New York (SUNY) Buffalo is currently proposing to move its medical, dental, nursing, pharmacy, and public health schools into downtown Buffalo and expand its campuses not only to meet its aspirations of becoming a national leader in education and research but also to act as an economic catalyst for a host city that has experienced significant economic decline in the past few decades. Accomplishing this would require state legislative approval for tuition increases and public–private partnerships to pay for the expansions (Kaplan, 2011).

For city administrators, having a top-tier higher education institution located in their municipality can mean an increase in jobs, revenue, and quality of life for their community. Universities can provide a municipality with a venue where public events can be held as well as educational opportunities for its citizens. A successful economic relationship can enable both entities to obtain outside funding or cut costs on joint projects and operational tasks. In short, a higher reputation for an institution can benefit its host municipality.

Institutional research offices are well positioned to obtain the data necessary to analyze the relationship between top-tier institutions and their host municipalities. Institutional research offices already conduct policy analyses by benchmarking their institution against other institutions with similar characteristics or that have qualities that the institution aspires to obtain. Upper administrators then use these comparisons to establish policies that, for example, will improve graduation rates through better student selection or encourage more faculty research through targeted hiring. Benchmark metrics gathered by institutional research offices can enable university administrators to gain support from political constituencies as well as the university community when proposing new policies. An institutional research office would only need to add municipal data to institutional characteristics that have already been mined for other benchmarking purposes.

The purpose of this research is to analyze the attributes of top-tier public institutions and their host municipalities to determine if there are common factors in how the organizations are structured, how they interact, and whether a symbiotic relationship exists that can benefit both entities. This research attempted to determine if cities under a certain population size will be more correlated to a top-tier university, and thus more dependent on that university as an economic driver, than a city with a much larger population or one with a more diverse economic portfolio (for example, Burlington, Vermont, as opposed to Seattle, Washington). The research also investigated whether smaller cities that demonstrate economic dependency on their higher education institutions are also more likely to have joint city–university programs than larger cities whose economies are more independent from their higher education institutions. The research then attempted to confirm whether a relationship with the host municipality enables a university to move up in the USNWR rankings or if there are other benefits that can be obtained if both municipal and university administrators seek certain common goals. With the data obtained in this study, it is hoped that areas of cooperation will be discovered that can assist administrators in municipalities and higher education institutions in setting goals that are obtainable and realistic and that will propel a higher education institution upward in the rankings.

The results of this research were then applied to seven "emerging" Texas public research universities as defined by the Texas state legislature to determine if the characteristics of host municipalities are predictive of the success of emerging public universities in Texas in attaining top-tier status. If a correlation can be found, then perhaps this research might be able to provide suggestions on how best to concentrate efforts toward attaining improved conditions and greater synergy between the emerging research institution and its host municipality.

Literature Review

A review of scholastic work on universities and their relationship to municipalities indicates that there has not been a significant amount of research on the connection between city services, universities, and efforts to improve university standing in USNWR rankings. Even the connection between universities and the use of municipal services has not received a great deal of attention beyond discussions of city complaints that universities are tax-exempt entities that impact service delivery. However, this does not mean that there has not been ample research on town–gown relations. There has been a significant amount of work demonstrating the historical ties (some as far back as the medieval era) between cities and universities (Barzun, 1968; Bender, 1988; McGirr, Kull, and Enns, 2003; Mosher, 1975). Much of the literature over the past twenty years tends to focus on the conflicts that emerge between cities and universities regarding tax exemption, the need for payment in lieu of taxes (PILOT) or services in lieu of taxes (SILOT), and hostility from cities to university expansion plans (Fischer, 2010; Healy, 1995). Recently, these arguments have been used as a starting point for calls for closer cooperation between cities and universities so that they may mutually benefit each other (Bender, 1998; Freeland, 2005; Kysiak, 1986; Maurrasse, 2001; O'Mara, 2010; Sungu-Eryilmaz, 2009).

There is sufficient research demonstrating how the university is a contributor to economic development, a key partner in neighborhood rejuvenation and a necessity for any city trying to adapt to the new knowledge-based economy (Aaron and Watson, 2008; Baker-Minkel, Moody, and Kieser, 2004; Bok, 2003; Booth and Jarrett, 1976; Fischer, 2006; Hewlett, 2004; Initiative for a Competitive Inner City, 2002; Mayer, 2008; Perry and Wiewel, 2005; Rodin, 2007; Steinkamp, 1998; Trani and Holsworth, 2010; Watson, 1995). Aside from the economic impact, some research has been dedicated to the nature of college towns as a unique type of city in modern America (Gumprecht, 2003). Other researchers have explored the capacity for universities to be facilitators of citizen involvement in government affairs (Kathi, Cooper, and Meek, 2007) and how the city officials can play a valuable role as educators in university classrooms (Booker, 2006; Milam, 2003). This brief survey of town–gown relations in academic literature should not be mistaken for being absolute in scope or depth, but merely to designate the predominant trends in the literature and indicate what has been left unexplored. To the authors' knowledge there has been no systemic work investigating the full range of city services that a university may use or have agreements with municipalities for usage. There has not been a model developed that categorizes the size/scope of cities and their respective universities or looks at the various agreements between cities and universities (services, easements, joint training). Finally, there has not been a discernable attempt in the literature to look at the potential relationship between city services and university growth.

Given that little research exists on the relationship between city services and universities, it should come as no surprise that there is no research that also includes the impact of USNWR rankings on universities and their efforts to increase their position in the rankings. Academic research on the USNWR rankings tends to focus on analyzing the quality of the rankings and, more often than not, making criticisms of the variables and formulas utilized to make the rankings (Brooks, 2005; Pike, 2004; Webster, 2001). Criticisms of the USNWR rankings also focus on their potential to disadvantage predominantly black colleges (Kamara, 2007) or to generate academic homogenization that is antithetical to the American university mission (Diver, 2005). Aside from the accuracy of the rankings as a tool for evaluating the university, a decent portion of the research looks at the impact of the rankings on universities on student enrollment and university reputation or as a litmus test for university success (Bastedo and Bowman, 2010; Meredith, 2004; Michael, 2005; Monks and Ehrenberg, 1999; Standifird, 2005). Despite the bevy of research on the USNWR rankings, even when looking at how they can drive university goals and policy, there has not been any academic work looking at universities wishing to improve their rankings and the relationship to city services that the municipality offers. Given the lack of research on a potential connection between city services, universities, and the need to achieve a higher ranking (such as tier one) from *U.S. News and World Report*, we conducted the following research project.

Methodology

The methodology for this research involves qualitative and quantitative techniques in gathering the data as well as quantitative techniques in the analysis portion of the research. The qualitative methodology portion of the research incorporated archival documentation such as published reports and information gathered online and, where documentation was unavailable, interviews of both university and city administrators (Leedy and Ormond, 2001; Webb, Campbell, Schwartz, and Sechrest, 2000). This research is a cross-sectional study. The list of top-tier public universities and the metrics collected and reported on those institutions was extracted directly from the USNWR website for academic year 2009–10. Census data and geospatial information provided population, socioeconomic, and geographical characteristics of both universities and their host communities. The list for the Texas emerging universities was taken from the Texas Higher Education Coordinating Board website.

Commonalities among top-ranked higher education institutions were identified in this study. Certain metrics such as graduation and retention rates, faculty quality, and research expenditures immediately identified some public universities as being of the highest quality and most successful in the United States. The characteristics of the host municipalities for these top-ranked institutions were then analyzed for key patterns in public transportation, form of city government, tax structure, demographics, and the local school district, to name a few. This research collected data for seventy-eight different variables in the areas of higher education institutional data, municipal data, and geospatial information system (GIS) data. (See Appendix A for a complete list of the variables used in the research.)

Do host municipalities share certain characteristics that make them particularly agreeable to top public universities, or does the presence of these universities affect the host municipality? If there is a correlation found between key metrics for top universities and their host municipalities, is there a causal relationship? This study attempted to address those questions during the analysis phase of the project. The methodology of this research was then applied to seven "emerging" Texas public research universities as defined by the Texas state legislature with the hope of determining if the characteristics of host municipalities are predictive of the success of emerging public universities in Texas in attaining top-tier status.

Data Analyses

According to the USNWR, universities are classified into four main groups: National Universities, National Liberal Arts Colleges, Regional Universities, and Regional Colleges. The researchers compared different characteristics of the municipalities by these four main university categories. The USNWR further classifies schools in the Regional Universities and Regional Colleges categories into one of four geographic regions: North, South, Midwest, and West. We will thus explore whether there are any differentials by location.

- Municipal characteristics (budget, number of employees)
- Median income (social economic status)
- Municipal budget (is there any allocation of this budget to the university?)
- Transport (access to an airport/rail, and so on)
- Municipal facilities on university land/next to university land
- Violent crime rate
- Form of government for the city
- Type of student housing
- Collaboration of municipalities with universities

To establish whether there are differences using each of the parameters above, the researchers performed a Students' t test for continuous variables comparing between two groups and an analysis of variance (ANOVA) for groups/categories with more than two groups (for example, total population). A chi-square test of independence was then used to assess associations between parameters that are categorical (for example, form of government for the city). We can further subdivide and classify universities into classes: 1–25, top universities; 26–50; 50–75; and bottom

25 universities for both national and regional universities. Using this approach, we then assessed for trends using a chi-square test for trend.

The USNWR criteria for ranking are based on a number of parameters that focus the institutional performance in a variety of perspectives. There are various challenges inherent in the classification of universities, that is, what parameters best discriminates among academic institutions, how many parameters should be included without overfitting and/or saturating the prognostic model used in determining the heterogeneity of universities ranging from subjects offered and also how to establish weights for the distinct parameters.

In order to establish which parameters of a municipality and weights are more appropriate for the determination of university ranking, we applied a multivariate analysis of the characteristics and demographics of the municipalities on which the universities reside. Using this approach, we identified which factors are largely responsible and contribute most to the ranking of universities. Statistical significance was assessed at the 5 percent level of significance (p value < 0.05). All analysis was performed by SPSS for Windows (Chicago, SPSS Inc.).

Results of Analyses

Population of Study (see Appendix B). A total of sixty-eight public, top-tier universities were used for this research. The researchers categorized the 2009 university rankings into classes of 10 (1–10, best universities; 11–20; 21–30; 31–40; 41–50; 51–60; and 61–68) for ease of comparison and analysis. The researchers assessed whether there were differences between university ranking and enrollment rates in fall 2009 (as can be seen in Table 7.1).

Analysis of University Variables (see Appendix B). The researchers assessed differences in enrollment rates by university ranking

Table 7.1. Analysis of Enrollment of Top-Tier Public Institutions

Rankings 2009	Fall Enrollment Rates Mean	International Enrollment Rates Mean	Out-of-State Undergraduate Enrollment Mean	Total
1–10	31,144.3	3,172.2	5,520.336	10
11–20	39,459	2,923.4	5,267.482	10
21–30	34,230.15	2,813.692	8,261.294	10
31–40	19,125.11	1,280.222	6,294.654	10
41–50	28,747	1,656.333	6,323.913	10
51–60	25,880.82	1,771.909	6,020.996	10
61–68	23,138.5	1,261.833	5,132.503	8
Total	29,491.09	2,220.956	6,262.766	68

(categorized into groups of ten) using ANOVA. For nonemerging public top-tier universities, the variables that were significant at the 0.05 level were total enrollment, percentage of international students enrolled, membership in the Association of American Universities, Carnegie Classification 2005, Carnegie Undergraduate Profile, Carnegie Enrollment Profile, presence of a law school, total revenues, total expenditures, research expenditures, and endowment value at fiscal year-end. Nine of the top ten best-ranked universities have law schools, and eight of the best 11–20 also had law schools (17/20 of the best twenty universities had a law school). Most universities in the top ranks were those that were involved in very high research activity. Of the number of universities that are involved in very high research, 31/52 (60 percent) universities are in the top thirty ranking compared to 21/52 (40 percent).

The number of tenure and on-track faculty, total instructional employees, total noninstructional employees, total campus community, the number of graduate assistants, and the number of bachelor's, master's, and doctoral degrees awarded were significant at the 0.05 level. Variables that demonstrated no significance to university ranking were as follows: percentage of undergraduates who were out of state (mean enrollment = 6,262.8), whether the university had a hospital, whether the university granted medical degrees, whether the university was a component of a university system or governed by a board of trustees, or whether it was in an NCAA division. Carnegie undergraduate instructional program, Carnegie graduate instruction program, Carnegie size and setting, Carnegie classification 2000, grant status, student or faculty/staff housing, number of first professional degrees awarded, and average alumni giving rate were also not significant to ranking.

However, several variables that were not significant to top-tier universities were for the emerging institutions. The percent of undergraduates that were out of state (mean enrollment = 814.8), whether the institution granted medical degrees, Carnegie graduate instructional program, Carnegie size and setting, Carnegie classification 2000, grant status, average alumni giving rate, whether governed by a board of trustees, and faculty/staff housing were significant at the 0.05 level. Variables that were significant to top-tier institutions but were not significant to emerging universities were total enrollment, percent of international students enrolled, presence of a law school, Carnegie enrollment profile, endowment value at fiscal year end, total campus community, and the number of bachelor's and master's degrees awarded. For both groups, the presence of a hospital, whether the institution was a component of a university system, Carnegie undergraduate instructional program, NCAA division, and number of first professional degrees awarded were not significant to institutional ranking. However, for both emerging and top-tier institutions, financial variables like revenues, expenditures, and research expenditures, and qualitative variables like Carnegie classification 2005, Carnegie undergraduate profile, tenured and on-track faculty, graduate assistants, membership in the Association of American Universities, total instructional and noninstructional employees, and doctoral degrees awarded were significant to their rankings.

There were differences in the characteristics between top-tier and emerging institutions. Unlike most top-tier universities, which have hospitals and grant medical degrees, none of the seven emerging universities have a hospital or grant medical degrees. Also, only two of the seven universities have law schools: the University of Houston and Texas Tech University. All of the emerging universities are a component in a university system and 85.7 percent (six out of seven) are classified as being high-research institutions according to the Carnegie classification of 2005. Of the seven emerging universities, four of them are classified as offering professional Arts and Sciences and three have a balanced Arts and Science professions. According to Carnegie enrollment profile, five of the emerging universities are classified as offering a high-profile undergraduate program, one with the majority being undergraduate programs, and one other university classified as offering a very high undergraduate program. According to Carnegie classification 2000, four of these universities are classified as offering extensive doctoral research programs, two with intensive doctoral research programs, and one primarily offering master's programs.

All of the emerging universities are large four-year institutions, with the majority of students being in-state residents who commute. Three of the universities are based in a metropolitan terrain, one in a metropolitan/coastal terrain, one in a metropolitan/riverine terrain, and two in the plains. Five of the emerging universities are based in an urban setting and two in a suburban area. Four of the institutions are based in large cities, compared to three that are in medium-sized cities. None of the seven emerging universities is a member of the Association of American Universities.

Analysis of Geographic Information System Variables (see Appendix C). Top-tier universities and Texas emerging universities were compared against the following Geographic Information System variables: state, city, university setting, degree of urbanization, geographic region, population, population density per state, median income, expansion ability for university, airport, rail, demographics of host city (Caucasian, African American, Hispanic, Asian), type of terrain, density per square mile, acres, square footage per student (calculated variable), square footage of campus, and square miles of campus. For top-tier institutions, the only two variables that were significant to their ranking were population and the number of Asian people who lived in the host city, with the latter variable being significant at the 0.05 level. However, for the emerging institutions, the variables that were significant were type of terrain, density per square mile, geographic region, and the number of Hispanic people who lived in the host city, with the last two variables being significant at the 0.05 level. This is most likely due to the unique geographic qualities of the state of Texas, where the bulk of the population—a substantial portion of which are Hispanic—live along the Interstate 35 corridor, on the coast, or along the Rio Grande River.

Analysis of Joint Variables for Higher Education Institutions and Municipalities (see Appendix D). Nine variables pertaining to joint projects or agreements between higher education institutions and their host municipalities were analyzed: existence of a comprehensive master plan integrated with the municipal plan, municipal agreements with the university, ranking of the university as a local employer, joint training, joint facilities, economic development, municipal deals with the university regarding utility rates, membership in the International Town and Gown Association, and whether the university is leasing land or granting easements to the city. The only variable that was significant for top-tier institutions was membership in the International Town and Gown Association. The International Town and Gown Association is a network of municipal leaders, practitioners, university officials, faculty, students, and citizens who collaborate on projects meant to improve the quality of life in their communities. It appears that membership in this organization indicates a high level of commitment by the university toward fostering a vibrant and functional community in and around the campus.

Although there was little connection between a university's ranking and the number of agreements with its host municipality, most top-tier universities (fifty-seven out of fifty-nine) maintained agreements with their respective municipalities. This high percentage suggests that most top-tier public universities and their host municipalities do find this type of arrangement mutually beneficial as seen in Table 7.2.

The value that municipalities assign to the presence of a public top-tier institution in their community can be seen in Table 7.3, where universities are ranked by their host municipalities based on the institution's importance as an employer in the community.

While it is not possible to perform a statistical analysis on some of the qualitative data, some examples can provide insight into how higher education institutions and host municipalities can work together to improve their organizational environments and services. One example can be seen at the Miami University at Ohio and the City of Oxford hosting joint

Table 7.2. Joint Variables for Public Top-Tier Institutions and Municipalities

Characteristic	Yes (%)	No (%)
Comprehensive master plan integrated with university	46 (67.6)	22 (32.4)
Municipal agreements with universities	57 (96.6)	2 (3.4)
University and municipal joint training	45 (86.5)	7 (13.5)
University and municipal economic development	40 (78.4)	10 (21.6)
University town and gown association	15 (20)	60 (80)
University leasing land or granting easements to city	36 (59)	25 (41)

Table 7.3. Rank of University as an Employer in the Municipality for Public Top-Tier Institutions

Rank	Frequency	Percentage
1	38	62.3
2	6	9.84
3	3	4.92
4	4	6.56
5	3	4.92
7	2	3.28
8	2	3.28
23	1	1.64
25	1	1.64
31	1	1.64

Table 7.4. Facilities Jointly Owned by Universities and Municipalities That Are Public Top-Tier Institutions

University and Municipal Joint Facilities	Frequency	Percentage
No	21	39.62
Yes	24	45.28
None	1	1.89
None listed	7	13.21

training exercises between the two organizations' police departments (City of Oxford, 2010). Such training arrangements benefit both organizations in how first responders can react to a situation and how both organizations can benefit from cost savings from having the police departments train at the same time.

Cost savings and improvement in service can also be realized in both joint economic development efforts and mutually funded facilities, which benefits the higher education institution as well as its host municipality. An example of these two types of activities can be seen with Ohio State University's redevelopment of the City of Columbus's heliport facility into a medical facility and the joint effort by both Columbus and Ohio State University to revitalize neighborhoods for economic development purposes (City of Columbus, 2010; Ohio State University Board of Regents, 1997). The University of Maryland at College Park is another example of a university that is attempting to improve cooperation with its host municipality in redevelopment efforts by assisting with certain civil engineering projects (that is, the Edmonston Stormwater Project) (University of Maryland, Office of Sustainability, 2009). Table 7.4 demonstrates that the majority of public top-tier institutions have joint facilities with their host municipalities.

Utility rates are another area where municipalities and higher education institutions frequently attempt to negotiate a set rate to benefit the higher education institution (Table 7.5).

Table 7.5. Top-Tier Public Institutions with Special Utility Rates from Host Municipalities

Municipal Deal With University Regarding Utility Rates	Frequency	Percentage
Not applicable (N/A)	9	16.36
No	34	61.82
Yes	12	21.82

Table 7.6. Joint Variables for Emerging Public Top-Tier Institutions and Municipalities

Characteristic	Yes (%)	No (%)
Comprehensive master plan integrated with university	5 (71.4)	2 (28.6)
Municipal agreements with universities	7 (100)	0 (0)
University and municipal joint training	5 (71.4)	2 (28.6)
University and municipal economic development	4 (57.1)	3 (42.9)
University town and gown association	0 (0)	7 (100)
University leasing land or granting easements to city	6 (85.7)	1 (14.3)

In addition, many universities have mutual aid arrangements with their host municipality. The University of Massachusetts at Amherst has a mutual aid agreement with the Town of Amherst that calls for resources to be allocated accordingly in times of crisis (University of Massachusetts at Amherst, 2011).

By benchmarking institutions that have these intercooperative arrangements, a best-practices approach can be formulated where such arrangements can be implemented within the constraints of available resources and where political realities will allow for such cooperation. Certainly, these practices can provide ideas for beneficial arrangements to other institutions that are aspiring to become a top-tier institution along with their host municipalities. These arrangements can provide improved services, cost savings, and organizational effectiveness to both higher education institutions and host municipalities. These cooperative arrangements may also enable an emerging university to cut costs or offset budget shortfalls.

Among emerging universities, the joint variables that were significant at the 0.05 level to an institution's ranking were a comprehensive master plan integrated with the municipality, municipal agreements with the universities, university and municipal economic development, and university leasing land or granting easements to the city. As seen in Table 7.6, five out of seven emerging institutions have joint training with their host cities, and three of the emerging universities have joint facilities with their host municipality.

Additionally, the presence of a municipal deal with the university regarding utility rates was significant at the 0.05 level. This would suggest that an emerging university's ranking is more closely connected to their host municipalities whereas the ranking of the top-tier institutions is somewhat decoupled from their cities. Is it possible that, as a university rises in prominence, it relies on the economic resources of its host municipality to attain higher rankings, or is the link between the ranking of Texas emerging institutions and the agreements they create with their municipalities the result of some factor unique to the state? Additional research would be required to answer this question. For higher education institutions that are seeking to become top-tier institutions, cooperation with their host municipality would appear to benefit both organizations in terms of effectiveness of operations, cost savings, and the ability to offer services to a broader community.

Municipality Variables (Appendix E). Ten municipality variables were analyzed to determine significance to university rankings: if the city provided utilities, transportation in the municipality, violent crime rate (2009), form of city government, the presence of an economic development corporation or department, state income tax, state sales tax, if the city adopted a general fund budget, educational attainment of city residents, and yearly budget for the school district. For top-tier institutions, none of these variables were significant (there was insufficient data regarding the yearly budget for the school district to make an analysis). However, for emerging institutions, utilities, violent crime rate, form of city government, an economic development corporation or department and the educational attainment of the city's residents were significant at the 0.05 level (a statistical test could not be performed for transportation in a municipality and for state sales tax). This would suggest that emerging institutions are more affected by the quality of life in their host municipalities than are top-tier public institutions.

A majority of the emerging universities (six out of seven) are based in cities where the form of government is represented by a city manager and a city mayor. Only one university is based in a city where it is governed by a city mayor only. None of the seven emerging universities has a deal with their municipality regarding utility rates except for the University of Texas at El Paso, where the city is investigating the possibility of creating a franchise fee to subsidize UTEP's energy costs associated with Tier-One Status efforts.

Conclusion

The research has demonstrated an association between public top-tier universities and their host municipalities. However, no data could be found to support the notion that certain arrangements or agreements between public top-tier universities and their host municipality would result in an increase in USNWR rankings. The research did discover that many cities and top-tier public universities see significant economic benefits in cooperating with economic development efforts, joint training, and integrated comprehensive master plans. Emerging institutions that are currently evaluating whether to enter into new joint agreements or expand upon existing ones may do well to proceed, if for no other reason than to realize a tangible financial benefit.

Many emerging universities are dependent on taxpayer-supported general funds to pay for utilities, building maintenance, and faculty salaries. Cooperative arrangements with host municipalities may enable an emerging university to cut overhead costs or offset budget shortfalls, thus allowing them to dedicate more of their general fund toward faculty salaries or other academic efforts. Many emerging universities are located in cities that could also be considered "emerging" with regard to economic diversity, educational attainment of their population, and quality of life. These municipalities benefit from cooperative agreements by offsetting their own budget shortfalls while enticing more educated citizens to live in their city. These citizens, in turn, pay higher taxes, which can be applied toward improving local schools, infrastructure, and recreational facilities. Better facilities can entice entrepreneurs who need well-educated workers to locate their businesses within these municipalities.

Top-tier institutions with low overhead and diversified revenue streams can maintain a certain level of independence, which in turn can allow them to invest in academic programs and student services that can attract top applicants and in research facilities that can bolster faculty recruitment. While many of the top-tier institutions are also located in cities known for being entrepreneur friendly and having a high quality of life, others are located in areas that have declined. The success of the top-tier institutions in attaining high USNWR rankings seems decoupled from their host municipalities' success as a community. Is this the result of some kind of organizational life cycle in which universities, once they achieve prominence, no longer need their host municipality to remain so? Or do these universities face a future decline as desirable applicants choose to enroll elsewhere and top faculty are lured away by communities with better schools, infrastructure, and recreational activities? And what of those communities that do not list their local top-tier institution as a key employer or who do not maintain many joint agreements? Could they continue to thrive economically if the university declined in quality or even ceased to exist? This research does not attempt to answer these questions, but future analysis might be able to offer some clarity on these issues.

APPENDIX A: VARIABLES USED IN STUDY

University Variables

1. Institution name
2. Fall 2009 total enrollment
3. International students enrolled
4. Percentage international
5. Percentage of undergraduates out of state
6. University has hospital
7. Grants medical degrees
8. University law school
9. Component of university system
10. System name
11. Carnegie Classification 2005 Basic
12. Carnegie Undergraduate Instructional Program
13. Carnegie Graduate Instructional Program
14. Carnegie Undergraduate Profile
15. Carnegie Enrollment Profile
16. Carnegie Size and Setting
17. Carnegie Classification 2000
18. Grant status
19. Association of American Universities
20. NCAA division
21. Total revenues FY2009
22. Total expenditures FY2009
23. Research expenditures FY2009
24. Endowment value at fiscal year-end 2009
25. Average alumni giving rate
26. Tenure/On-track faculty
27. Graduate assistants
28. Total instructional employees
29. Total noninstructional employees
30. Total campus community
31. % Student—calculated variable
32. % Instructional—calculated variable
33. % Staff—calculated variable
34. Bachelor's degrees awarded (AY09)
35. Master's degrees awarded (AY09)
36. Doctoral degrees awarded (AY09)
37. First professional degrees awarded (AY09)
38. Board of trustees
39. Type of student housing
40. Faculty/Staff housing

Geospatial Information System (GIS) Variables
1. State
2. City
3. University setting
4. Degree of urbanization
5. Geographic region
6. Population
7. Population density per state
8. Median income
9. Expansion ability for university
10. Airport
11. Rail
12. Demographics: Caucasian/African American/Hispanic/Asian
13. Type of terrain
14. Density per square mile
15. Acres
16. Square foot per student—calculated variable
17. Square feet campus
18. Square miles campus

Joint Variables for Higher Education Institutions and Municipalities
1. Comprehensive master plan integrated with municipal
2. Municipal agreements with universities
3. Rank of university as an employer
4. University and municipal joint training
5. University and municipal joint facilities
6. University and municipal economic development
7. Municipal deal with university with regards to utility rates
8. University advertised on city website
9. International Town and Gown Association
10. University leasing land or granting easements to city

Municipality Variables
1. Provide utilities
2. Transportation in municipality
3. Violent crime rate 2009
4. Form of government for city
5. Economic development corporation or department
6. State income tax
7. State sales tax
8. Adopted general fund budget
9. Educational attainment of residents
10. Yearly budget for school district

NEW DIRECTIONS FOR INSTITUTIONAL RESEARCH • DOI: 10.1002/ir

APPENDIX B

Statistical ANOVA Tests on Variables for Nonemerging Top-Tier Public Universities

University Variables	p Value
1. Fall 2009 total enrollment	0.008
2. Percentage of international students enrolled	0.008
3. Percentage of undergraduates out of state	0.77
4. University has hospital	0.08
5. Grants medical degrees	0.79
6. University law school	0.01
7. Component of university system	0.29
8. Carnegie Classification 2005	0.005
9. Carnegie Undergraduate Instructional Program	0.30
10. Carnegie Graduate Instructional Program	0.30
11. Carnegie Undergraduate Profile	0.002
12. Carnegie Enrollment Profile	0.002
13. Carnegie Size and Setting	0.09
14. Carnegie Classification 2000	0.17
15. Grant status	0.08
16. Association of American Universities	<0.001
17. NCAA division	>0.05
18. Total revenues FY2009	<0.01
19. Total expenditures FY2009	<0.01
20. Research expenditures FY2009	<0.01
21. Endowment value at fiscal year-end 2009	<0.01
22. Average alumni giving rate	0.38
23. Tenure/On-track faculty	<0.05
24. Graduate assistants	<0.05
25. Total instructional employees	<0.05
26. Total noninstructional employees	<0.05
27. Total campus community	<0.05
28. Bachelor's degrees awarded (AY09)	<0.05
29. Master's degrees awarded (AY09)	<0.05
30. Doctoral degrees awarded (AY09)	<0.05
31. First professional degrees awarded (AY09)	>0.05
32. Board of trustees	0.59
33. Type of student housing	>0.05
34. Faculty/Staff housing	0.34

Note: Statistical significance was assessed at the 5 percent level of significance (p value < 0.05).

Statistical ANOVA Tests on Variables for Emerging Top-Tier Public Universities

University Variables	p Value
1. Fall 2009 total enrollment	0.76
2. Percentage of international students enrolled	0.91
3. Percentage of undergraduates out of state	0.003
4. University has hospital	0.17
5. Grants medical degrees	0.005
6. University law school	0.09
7. Component of university system	0.10
8. Carnegie Classification 2005	<0.001
9. Carnegie Undergraduate Instructional Program	0.56
10. Carnegie Graduate Instructional Program	0.02
11. Carnegie Undergraduate Profile	<0.001
12. Carnegie Enrollment Profile	0.55
13. Carnegie Size and Setting	0.002
14. Carnegie Classification 2000	0.05
15. Grant status	<0.001
16. Association of American Universities	0.013
17. NCAA division	0.29
18. Total revenues FY2009	0.02
19. Total expenditures FY2009	0.02
20. Research expenditures FY2009	0.011
21. Endowment value at fiscal year-end 2009	0.15
22. Average alumni giving rate	<0.001
23. Tenure/On-track faculty	0.01
24. Graduate assistants	0.03
25. Total instructional employees	0.01
26. Total noninstructional employees	0.03
27. Total campus community	0.35
28. Bachelor's degrees awarded (AY09)	0.38
29. Master's degrees awarded (AY09)	0.68
30. Doctoral degrees awarded (AY09)	0.02
31. First professional degrees awarded (AY09)	0.80
32. Board of trustees	<0.001
33. Type of student housing	N/A
34. Faculty/Staff housing	0.001

Note: Statistical significance was assessed at the 5 percent level of significance (p value < 0.05).

APPENDIX C

Statistical ANOVA Tests on Variables for Nonemerging Public Top-Tier Universities—GIS

Geospatial Information System (GIS) Variables	p Value
1. State	NA
2. City	NA
3. University setting	>0.05
4. Degree of urbanization	>0.05
5. Geographic region	>0.05

Statistical ANOVA Tests on Variables for Nonemerging Public Top-Tier Universities—GIS (Continued)

Geospatial Information System (GIS) Variables	p Value
6. Population	0.02
7. Population density per state	>0.05
8. Median income	>0.05
9. Expansion ability for university	>0.05
10. Airport	>0.05
11. Rail	>0.05
12. Demographics: Caucasian	>0.05
African American	>0.05
Hispanic	>0.05
Asian	0.002
13. Type of terrain	>0.05
14. Density per square mile	>0.05
15. Acres	>0.05
16. Square foot per student—calculated variable	>0.05
17. Square feet campus	>0.05
18. Square miles campus	>0.05

Note: Statistical significance was assessed at the 5 percent level of significance (p value < 0.05).

Statistical ANOVA Tests on Variables for Emerging Public Top-Tier Universities—GIS

Geospatial Information System (GIS) Variables	p Value
1. State	N/A
2. City	N/A
3. University setting	0.33
4. Degree of urbanization	0.62
5. Geographic region	<0.001
6. Population	N/A
7. Population density per state	N/A
8. Median income	0.75
9. Expansion ability for university	0.56
10. Airport	0.12
11. Rail	0.18
12. Demographics: Caucasian	0.31
African American	0.68
Hispanic	<0.001
Asian	0.55
13. Type of terrain	0.03
14. Density per square mile	0.05
15. Acres	0.31
16. Square foot per student—calculated variable	0.67
17. Square feet campus	0.31
18. Square miles campus	0.31

Note: Statistical significance was assessed at the 5 percent level of significance (p value < 0.05).

NEW DIRECTIONS FOR INSTITUTIONAL RESEARCH • DOI: 10.1002/ir

APPENDIX D

Statistical ANOVA Tests on Joint Variables—Higher Education Institutions and Municipalities—Top-Tier Nonemerging Public Universities

Joint Variables for Higher Education Institutions and Municipalities	p Value
1. Comprehensive master plan integrated with municipal	>0.05
2. Municipal agreements with universities	0.84
3. Rank of university as an employer	0.21
4. University and municipal joint training	0.48
5. University and municipal joint facilities	0.34
6. University and municipal economic development	0.84
7. Municipal deal with university with regards to utility rates	0.62
8. International Town and Gown Association	0.003
9. University leasing land or granting easements to city	>0.05

Note: Statistical significance was assessed at the 5 percent level of significance (p value < 0.05).

Statistical ANOVA Tests on Joint Variables—Higher Education Institutions and Municipalities—Top-Tier Emerging Public Universities

Joint Variables for Higher Education Institutions and Municipalities	p Value
1. Comprehensive master plan integrated with municipal	<0.001
2. Municipal agreements with universities	0.02
3. Rank of university as an employer	0.07
4. University and municipal joint training	0.61
5. University and municipal joint facilities	0.77
6. University and municipal economic development	<0.001
7. Municipal deal with university with regards to utility rates	0.05
8. International Town and Gown Association	0.33
9. University leasing land or granting easements to city	0.001

Note: Statistical significance was assessed at the 5% level of significance (p value < 0.05).

APPENDIX E

Statistical ANOVA Tests Variables—Municipalities—Nonemerging Public Top-Tier Universities

Municipality Variables	p Value
1. Provide utilities	>0.05
2. Transportation in municipality	>0.05
3. Violent crime rate 2009	>0.05
4. Form of government for city	>0.05
5. Economic development corporation or department	>0.05
6. State income tax	>0.05
7. State sales tax	>0.05

Statistical ANOVA Tests Variables—Municipalities—Nonemerging Public Top-Tier Universities (Continued)

Municipality Variables	p Value
8. Adopted general fund budget	>0.05
9. Educational attainment of residents	>0.05
10. Yearly budget for school district	NA

Note: Statistical significance was assessed at the 5 percent level of significance (p value < 0.05).

Statistical ANOVA Tests Variables—Municipalities—Emerging Public Top-Tier Universities

Municipality Variables	p Value
1. Provide utilities	<0.001
2. Transportation in municipality	N/A
3. Violent crime rate 2009	0.007
4. Form of government for city	<0.001
5. Economic development corporation or department	0.001
6. State income tax	N/A
7. State sales tax	N/A
8. Adopted general fund budget	0.39
9. Educational attainment of residents	<0.001
10. Yearly budget for school district	N/A

Note: Statistical significance was assessed at the 5% level of significance (p value < 0.05).

References

Aaron, K., and Watson, D. J. "Networking in Economic Development: The Case of Project Emmitt." In D. J. Watson and J. C. Morris (eds.), Building the Local Economy: Cases in Economic Development. Athens, Ga.: Carl Vinson Institute of Government, 2008.

Baker-Minkel, K., Moody, J., and Kieser, W. "Town Gown." Economic Development Journal, 2004, 3(4), 7–15.

Bastedo, M. N., and Bowman, N. A. "U.S. News and World Report College Rankings: Modeling Institutional Effects on Organizational Reputation." American Journal of Education, 2010, 116(2), 163–183.

Barzun, J. The American University: How It Runs, Where It Is Going. New York: Harper and Row, 1968.

Bender, T. (ed.). The University and the City: From Medieval Origins to the Present. New York: Oxford University Press, 1988.

Bender, T. "Scholarship, Local Life, and the Necessity of Worldliness." In Herman Van der Wusten (ed.), The Urban University and Its Identity: Roots, Locations, Roles. Dordrecht, Netherlands: Kluwer Academic Publishers, 1998.

Bok, D. Universities in the Marketplace: The Commercialization of Higher Education. Princeton, N.J.: Princeton University Press, 2003.

Booker, S. L. "From the Classroom to the Council Chamber: How Town–Gown Collaborations Can Support Citizen Leadership." National Civic Review, 2006, 95(4), 37–42.

Booth, G. G., and Jarrett, J. E. "The Identification and Estimation of a University's Economic Impacts." Journal of Higher Education, 1976, 47(5), 565–576.

Brooks, R. "Measuring University Quality." *Review of Higher Education*, 2005, 29(1), 1–21.

City of Columbus. "Mayor's Biography." 2010. Retrieved December 1, 2010, from http://mayor.columbus.gov/biography.aspx?id=1456&menu_id=442.

City of Oxford. "City of Oxford." 2010. Retrieved October 1, 2010, from http://www.cityofoxford.org/.

Dallas Morning News. "Editorial: David Daniel, Finalist for Texas of the Year." December 23, 2009. Retrieved November 5, 2010, from www.danbranch.com/media/DallasMorningNews/dmn_20091223.htm.

Daniel, D. E. "Thoughts on Creating More Tier One Universities in Texas." Executive Summary, May 28, 2008. Retrieved November 5, 2010, from www.senate.state.tx.us/75r/senate/commit/c535/20080723/David_Daniel_Tier_One_Executive_Summary.pdf.

Diver, C. "Is There Life After Rankings?" *Atlantic Monthly*, November 2005.

Fischer, K. "The University as Economic Savior." *Chronicle of Higher Education*, 2006. Retrieved February 2, 2011, from http://chronicle.com/article/The-University-As-Economic/7492/.

Fischer, K. "Debate Over Taxes Sullies Town–Gown Relations in Pittsburgh; Higher Education Helped Save Pittsburgh, So Why Are the Two Sides Still Fighting?" *Chronicle of Higher Education*, 2010, 56(21). Retrieved on November 5, 2012, from http://chronicle.com/article/Debate-Over-Taxes-Sullies/63795/.

Freeland, R. M. "Universities and Cities Need to Rethink Their Relationship." *Chronicle of Higher Education*, 2005, 51(36). Retrieved on November 5, 2012, from http://chronicle.com/article/UniversitiesCities-Need/31692/.

Gumprecht, B. "The American College Town." *Geographical Review*, 2003, 93(1), 51–80.

Healy, P. "College vs. Communities." *Chronicle of Higher Education*, 1995, 41(34), A27–A32.

Hewlett, R. "In Plain Sight." *Economic Development Journal*, 2004, 3(4), 33–39.

Initiative for a Competitive Inner City (ICIC). *Leveraging Colleges and Universities for Urban Economic Development: An Action Agenda*. Boston: CEOs for Cities, 2002.

Kamara, M. "Are U.S. News' Rankings Inherently Biased Against Black Colleges?" *Diverse Issues in Higher Education*, 2007, 24(10), 8.

Kaplan, T. "In Buffalo, Visions, Perhaps Illusions, of a University-Fueled Revitalization." *New York Times*, May 8, 2011. Retrieved May 10, 2011, from www.nytimes.com/2011/05/09/nyregion/buffalo-pins-hope-for-revival-on-university-expansion.html?_r=2andemc=eta1.

Kathi, P. C., Cooper, T. L., Meek, J. W. "The Role of the University as a Mediating Institution in Neighborhood Council–City Agency Collaboration." *Journal of Public Affairs Education*, 2007, 13(2), 365–382.

Kysiak, R. C. "The Role of the University in Public–Private Partnerships." *Proceedings of the Academy of Political Science*, 1986, 36(2), 47–59.

Leedy, P. D., and Ormond, J. E. *Practical Research: Planning and Design*. (7th ed.) Upper Saddle River, N.J.: Prentice Hall, 2001.

Maurrasse, D. J. *Beyond the Campus: How Colleges and Universities Form Partnerships With Their Communities*. New York: Routledge, 2001.

Mayer, H. "Competition for High-Tech Jobs in Second-Tier Regions: The Case of Portland, Oregon." In D. J. Watson and J. C. Morris (eds.), *Building the Local Economy: Cases in Economic Development*. Athens, Ga.: Carl Vinson Institute of Government, 2008.

McGirr, D., Kull, R., and Enns, K. S. "Town and Gown." *Economic Development Journal*, 2003, 2(2), 16–24.

Meredith, M. "Why Do Universities Compete in the Ratings Game? An Empirical Analysis of the Effects of the 'U.S. News and World Report' College Rankings." *Research in Higher Education*, 2004, 45(5), 443–461.

Michael, S. O. "The Cost of Excellence: The Financial Implications of Institutional Rankings." *International Journal of Educational Management*, 2005, 19(5), 365–382.

Milam, D. M. "Practitioner in the Classroom: Bringing Local Government Experience Into the Public Administration Curriculum." *Public Administration Review*, 2003, *63*(3), 364–369.

Monks, J., and Ehrenberg, R. G. "*U.S. News and World Report*'s College Rankings: Why They Do Matter." *Change*, 1999, *31*(6), 42–51.

Mosher, F. C. *American Public Administration: Past, Present, Future*. Tuscaloosa, Ala.: University of Alabama Press, 1975.

O'Mara, M. P. "Beyond Town and Gown: University Economic Engagement and the Legacy of the Urban Crisis." *Journal of Technology Transfer*, 2010. Retrieved February 20, 2011, from http://www.scopus.com/record/display.url?eid=2-s2.0-84858443800&origin=inward&txGid=zazfsQrktED0_aELEJ8DqM6%3a1.

Ohio State University Board of Regents. "The University Neighborhoods Revitalization Plan." 1997. Retrieved December 1, 2010, from http://campuspartners.osu.edu/index.php/homeownership-incentives/osu-trustees-approves.

Perry, D. C., and Wiewel, W. *The University as Urban Developer: Case Studies and Analysis*. Armonk, N.Y.: ME Sharpe, 2005.

Pike, G. R. "Measuring Quality: A Comparison of U.S. News Rankings and NSSE Benchmarks." *Research in Higher Education*, 2004, *45*(2), 193–208.

Pope, J. "Clemson Official: School Manipulated Rankings." *USA Today*, June 7, 2009. Retrieved November 5, 2010, from http://usatoday30.usatoday.com/news/education/2009-06-04-clemson-rankings_N.htm.

Rodin, J. *University and Urban Revival: Out of the Ivory Tower and into the Streets*. Philadelphia: University of Pennsylvania Press, 2007.

Standifird, S. S. "Reputation Among Peer Academic Institutions: An Investigation of the *U.S. News and World Report*'s Rankings." *Corporate Reputation Review*, 2005, *8*(3), 233–244.

Steinkamp, J. "Reshaping Town–Gown Relations." *Connection: New England's Journal of Higher Education and Economic Development*, 1998, *13*(1), 24–28.

Sungu-Eryilmaz, Y. *Town-Gown Collaboration in Land Use and Development*. (Policy Focus Report). Cambridge, Mass.: Lincoln Institute of Land Policy, June 2009.

Texas Higher Education Coordinating Board, 2009. "Overview: HB 51, 81st Texas Legislature." July 2009. Retrieved on November 5, 2010, from http://www.thecb.state.tx.us/reports/PDF/1842.PDF.

Trani, E. P., and Holsworth, R. D. *The Indispensible University: Higher Education, Economic Development and the Knowledge Economy*. Lanham, Md.: Rowman & Littlefield, 2010.

University of Maryland, Office of Sustainability. "East Campus Redevelopment Project Sustainability Perspectives." 2009. Retrieved May 10, 2011, from www.eastcampus.umd.edu/EastCampusSustainabilityPerspectives.pdf.

University of Massachusetts—Amherst, 2011. "The University of Massachusetts—Amherst." Retrieved on March 10, 2011, from http://umass.edu/.

Watson, D. J. *The New Civil War*. Westport, Conn.: Praeger, 1995.

Webb, E. J., Campbell, D. T., Schwartz, R. D., and Sechrest, L. *Unobtrusive Measures*. Thousand Oaks, Calif.: Sage Classics, 2000.

Webster, T. J. "A Principal Component Analysis of the *U.S. News and World Report* Tier Rankings of Colleges and Universities." *Economics of Education Review*, 2001, *20*(3), 235–244.

NICOLAS A. VALCIK is an Associate Director for the Office of Strategic Planning and Analysis at the University of Texas at Dallas.

KIMBERLY E. SCRUTON is an Assistant Professor of Business Management at Methodist University.

STUART B. MURCHISON is a Clinical Associate Professor of Geography Geospatial Sciences at the University of Texas at Dallas.

TED J. BENAVIDES is an Executive in Residence for Public Affairs at the University of Texas at Dallas.

TODD JORDAN is a Doctoral Candidate in Public Affairs at the University of Texas at Dallas.

ANDREA D. STIGDON is an Administrative Services Officer in the Office of Strategic Planning and Analysis at the University of Texas at Dallas.

ANGELA M. OLSZEWSKI is the Chair for the Arlington, Massachusetts, Committee on Tourism and Economic Development.

8

This chapter discusses the methodological and statistical challenges in selecting appropriate peer institutions for benchmarking.

Taming Multivariate Data: Conceptual and Methodological Issues

Lawrence J. Redlinger, John J. Wiorkowski, Anna I. Moses

The purpose of this chapter is to discuss the conceptual, methodological, and statistical challenges in selecting appropriate peer institutions for comparative purposes. Our approach embraces a Western scientific tradition that physical things and phenomena can be *reduced into a set of key variables—identifiable parts—that make key contributions, and that the behavior of the whole—in this case institutions of higher education—can be understood by knowing the parts and how they contribute (behave).* Furthermore, a value is placed on *efficiency* and *effective (successful) outcomes (however defined).* These assumptions have spawned a number of models that stress in varying degrees the larger environmental, *structural and/ or contextual variables and "inputs-processes-outputs."* Input-processes-outputs models are central to comparative analyses in general and benchmarking in particular.[1] Figure 8.1 provides a representation of a general benchmarking model. This point of view frames the conceptual and methodological issues and the technique of principal components analysis we discuss in this chapter.

People-Processing Institutions

The tricky part for education is that institutions process people (not things) and are expected to change them for the better (Wheeler, 1966). The "inputs" arrive as sentient creatures with their own agendas, interact

NEW DIRECTIONS FOR INSTITUTIONAL RESEARCH, no. 156, Winter 2012 © Wiley Periodicals, Inc.
Published online in Wiley Online Library (wileyonlinelibrary.com) • DOI: 10.1002/ir.20033

Figure 8.1. The Benchmarking Model

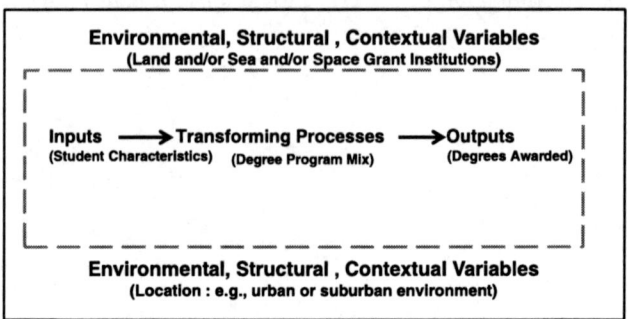

(are processed) by people following (more or less) institutionalized procedures (for example, coursework, tests, grades), are transformed (or not), and are released either as certified successes or not (drop-outs, stop-outs, flunk-outs). The institutionalized processes are embedded within a complex organization, which, when bundled together, forms the institution. The institution's inputs, characteristics, processes, outputs, and organizational environment can be more or less like others. The more similar institutions are along these dimensions, the more likely they are peers—that is, equal to each other or part of a group that shares the chosen characteristics.

Who's in the Universe?

Figuring out whom to include in the dataset is a matter of definition. One place to start is with the Integrated Postsecondary Education Data System (IPEDS); another is the Carnegie Foundation for the Advancement of Teaching (2012). In this chapter, we will use data from IPEDS to illustrate the problem with figuring out whom to include (Knapp, Kelly-Reid, and Ginder, 2012).

IPEDS participation is required for "institutions and administrative offices (central or system offices) that participate in Title IV federal student financial aid programs, such as Pell grants or Stafford loans." By this definition, there were 7,173 institutions and 80 administrative offices in the United States and other jurisdictions expected to report to IPEDS in the spring of 2011. These included four-year universities and colleges, two-year institutions, and non-degree-granting institutions (for example, schools of cosmetology) (Knapp, Kelly-Reid, and Ginder, 2012, p. 1).

In the fall of 2010, IPEDS reports that Title IV institutions enrolled 21.6 million students. Over 15 million, or about 71 percent, were enrolled in public institutions, 18 percent in private nonprofit institutions, and the remainder in the private for-profit sector. Sixty-two percent or 13.3 million were enrolled in four-year institutions and 36 percent or 7.8 million were enrolled in two-year institutions. The remaining 1.9 million were enrolled in less-than-two-year institutions. Fifty-nine percent of the students enrolled in public four-year institutions and 29 percent in private not-for-profit four-year institutions. The residual 12 percent were enrolled in private for-profit four-year institutions (Knapp, Kelly-Reid, and Ginder, 2012, pp. 7–8).

The institutions that train, school, and/or educate these students vary widely. They vary in their missions, in how they are governed and administered, in their institutional organization and processes, in their demographic characteristics, and in their larger organizational environment. The students that apply to, are admitted to, and actually matriculate are also highly variable. Furthermore, recruitment of students is quite variable. It can occur exclusively by cohort and be highly selective and time dependent (it happens only once a year). In contrast, recruitment can be singular and open to all, and matriculation occurs whenever the student wishes to begin taking a course (for example, on the Internet). Institutions can mix and match processes having hybrid selection processes that vary by program. Highly selective, time-dependent, cohort-based institutions with a high demand for admission and great emphasis on first-time undergraduates (all else being equal) are likely to use these *inclusion/exclusion* rules a priori to establish who they think is within the comparative population.

The Carnegie Foundation for the Advancement of Teaching (2012) provides another set of inclusion/exclusion rules. Starting with a universe of 4,633 institutions, Carnegie, in their basic classification schema, initially splits out two-year institutions from four-year, special focus, and tribal colleges. They further classify four-year institutions by highest degree awarded, and have specialized classification rules for baccalaureate, master's, and doctoral-granting institutions. For "Doctorate Granting Institutions" Carnegie utilizes a principal components analysis (discussed below) to sort institutions into three categories: those with very high research activity, those with high research activity, and a residual category of research university. Carnegie has other inclusion/exclusion classification rules for enrollment profiles, size and setting, undergraduate instructional programs, and others.

Teeter and Brinkman (1987, 1992) offer a typology of four non–mutually exclusive comparison groups. They argue that each can "play a legitimate role in informing decision-making, depending upon the situation" (1992, p. 65) by which we interpret them to mean *depending on "what is the question and who is asking?"* The four types are: competitors, aspiration, peer, and predetermined. Predetermined is further subdivided into natural, traditional, jurisdictional, and classification-based (Teeter and Brinkman, 1992). So if you are interested in NCAA Division 1-A schools (a natural predetermined grouping, in their terms), your selection process and inclusion rule would be different from (but not necessarily mutually exclusive from) an interest in competitors (defined as institutions that compete with one another for students or faculty or resources (Teeter and Brinkman, 1992, p. 65).

Trainer (2008) provides a useful overview of how to choose comparative groups and where to find and how to access comparative data. He notes that all selection rules (ala Teeter and Brinkman above) have strengths and weaknesses and observes that "it is important to take care in selecting, employing, and presenting institutions that may be used for comparative purposes" (Trainer, 2008, p. 23). Ultimately, the institutions included in the universe (actually a sample) *should* depend on the question being asked.

Clarifying the Question: What Is the Purpose and Who Wants to Know?

It is not surprising that quite a bit of discussion centers around which institutions to include and why, or that, under the variant conditions briefly mentioned earlier, many institutions believe that their cluster of characteristics, student populations, and so on make them unique and virtually not comparable. For some, benchmarking seems to be a politically charged, sensitive issue with high stakes. Yet, irrespective of these discussions and perceptions, comparisons and benchmarking abound. There is a rich literature on institutional comparisons and benchmarking.[7] Boards of regents want to know "who are we like?" State regulatory agencies desire metrics on tuition, graduation rates, and a host of other characteristics. That the undertaking is fraught with tricky twists and turns, methodological cliffs, and measurement issues may or may not bother regents and/or policymakers who are asking questions. In the final analysis, they simply want answers.[3] But, often, the question being asked turns into multiple questions and turns out to be complex and designed to serve multiple needs and stakeholders. For example, Terenzini, Hartmark, Lorang, and Shirley (1980) described the "administrative purposes" they addressed at the State University of New York (SUNY) at Albany. Their concern was with establishing a set of

> higher educational institutions that might reasonably be considered 'peers' of SUNY-Albany and with which it might be compared on such variables as faculty rank distributions and salaries, faculty workloads, and possibly, certain academic and research performance measures. Such comparisons are intended to serve directly the university's planning, budgeting and resource allocation processes" [p. 349].

Weeks, Puckett, and Daron (2000) explain how the Oregon University System selected peer groups with a mixed set of decision criteria that were attentive to the political considerations and technical issues involved in the selection. The "peers" would serve multiple purposes: budgeting, faculty compensation, performance measurements, and overtime trends.

Also, they would need to reflect the unique and distinctive missions of the individual institutions in the system (Weeks, Puckett, and Daron, 2000, p. 3) and have campus participation.

Merrill and Stanley (2010) describe their approach to selecting peers for the University of Hawaii at Manoa as an evidence-based strategy. While their peers were to be used for multiple purposes (inform policy; recruitment/retention of faculty, staff, and students; inform salary adjustments and teaching loads; and benchmark tuition schedules and budget alignment), they framed their research question more simply to what institutions were most similar to theirs? They whittled (filtered) the IPEDS universe from over 7,100 institutions to 63 using a priori exclusion rules (Merrill and Stanley, 2010).

So the general idea is to establish a set of similar institutions based on a set of characteristics that allow for comparisons at a point in time or over a defined time period. Institutions can, theoretically, use their similarities and differences to illustrate their achievements in the context of the selected institutions (generically "peers"). Furthermore, they can examine the set of identified institutions to see how they address problems that may be common to the entire set. Boards of regents and/or coordinating boards can also access the results and set policy objectives. Note, however, that it is critical to clearly frame the question, to have a clear statement for the purpose of comparison or benchmarking. In general, the more complex the question(s) become in terms of multiple uses the answers are to serve, the more variables one is tempted to include, which makes the methodology more problematic and analysis more complicated. Appropriate benchmarking groups—and the variables benchmarked—should vary based on what the specific question is and the purpose for which the exercise is undertaken. Lack of clarity in framing the question coupled with too many variables (the kitchen sink approach) seldom escapes calamity.

Variable Selection and Specification Issues

Choosing variables is one of the most significant steps that, as we noted earlier, cannot be achieved if you have not clearly framed the question. As Borden (2005) observes, variable selection "should be guided by an explicit theory or at least solid reasoning." He goes on to note:

> For example, the specification of peer institutions will vary widely depending on what characteristics are considered. It is imperative that the research sufficiently describes the rationale for selecting input characteristics, as well as limitations inherent in any specific set [p. 150].

The general underlying model specifies that inputs are subjected to transformative processes which yield outputs. The process is surrounded by, but also permeated by, environmental, structural, and contextual factors. Areas of interest to policymakers are often the efficiency of the production process and/or the effectiveness of the outcomes. Once the question is (clearly) specified, it is possible to choose variables that are just environmental, structural, or contextual variables (private institutions with no medical school in an urban setting) to arrive at the answer (see, for example, Teeter and Christal, 1984, pp. 2–4). Alternatively, you can start with picking institutions that achieve similar outputs (say graduation rates) and look for what your institution has in common with them. Or you can chose variables that represent inputs and/or transformative processes (degree programs available), or a mixture of all of these. There are pluses and minuses to all these approaches.

The richness of IPEDS, Carnegie, and other databases can lure researchers into adding more and more variables. Most often, the variables added are not capturing independent dimensions of the inputs, process, or outcomes. That is, they are often highly correlated with each other. We advise that, rather than add variables (the "kitchen sink" approach), researchers should clarify their purpose. If one is measuring student characteristics, what are the two or three critical dimensions? One can start by taking measures of student characteristics and looking at how they are correlated. For example, SAT-25th and SAT-75th percentile scores are so highly correlated they are in effect the same variable. If one is measuring processes, a single measure of science, technology, engineering, and mathematics (STEM) degrees may be sufficient, or a measure of average faculty salaries, or a measure of instructional expenditures per FTE (but not necessarily all three). Merrill and Stanley (2010), for example, in their peer analysis for the University of Hawaii at Manoa ultimately used eight variables representing input (student) characteristics, institutional (transformative process) characteristics, and output (bachelor's degrees awarded) characteristics. In the model we demonstrate later in this chapter, we use seven variables to represent institutional characteristics and student characteristics. This model seeks to establish a set of similar institutions based on student (input) and institutional (transformative process) characteristics.

Proxy Variables and Weighting

As Weeks, Puckett, and Daron (2000) note, most benchmarking studies rely on IPEDS data; some make use of Carnegie Classification data, and still others use American Association of University Professors (AAUP) faculty salary data (see Terenzini, Hartmark, Lorang, and Shirley, 1980). Perhaps because IPEDS is readily available, outcomes (degrees awarded) data are often used as a proxy for the mix of programs (transformative processes) and the importance assigned to programs. Weeks, Puckett, and Daron (2000, pp. 4–5), for example, employ nineteen variables—three are categorical and sixteen are measures derived from IPEDS. Of the sixteen measures, thirteen, or 81 percent, are degrees awarded data.

NEW DIRECTIONS FOR INSTITUTIONAL RESEARCH • DOI: 10.1002/ir

Teeter and Brinkman (1992) describe the approach developed by the National Center for Higher Education Management Systems (NCHEMS). Their method combines contextual (categorical or classification) nominal variables with other data. The nominal, contextual variables (e.g., land grants) are used to "reduce the universe," and then other measures are utilized. Of the twenty measures they enumerate, thirteen, or 65 percent, are degrees awarded (outcome) variables (Teeter and Brinkman, 1992, p. 69).

It is important to recognize that degrees awarded data are: (1) imperfect proxy measures for program emphasis, and that (2) degrees awarded variables are often highly correlated with each other; they are not independent variables but often are measuring the same underlying element. Further, if one is interested in comparing how institutions with similar inputs have variations in outcomes, using outcome measures as proxy variables for institutional characteristics seems problematic.

Teeter and Christal (1984) address two different issues: variation in method and differences in variable specification. Not surprisingly, they find that different methodologies and differences in variable specification lead to dissimilar results. They note that the "purposes and desires of the home institution will determine which methodology might best serve its needs" (Teeter and Christal, 1984, p. 12).

Further, researchers often employ weighting schemes (see, for example, Teeter and Cristal, 1984; Teeter and Brinkman 1992; and Weeks, Puckett, and Daron, 2000). While there are sound logical reasons for weighting variables (see Weeks, Puckett, and Daron, 2000, p. 4) such as institution mission, a priori weighting is a policy decision. It is easier to apply such a scheme to a single institution (even though one might desire to run an analysis without weights first in order to see how weighting affects results). But are the weights appropriate for the components of a system (for example, SUNY) or for an entire sample of potential comparison institutions? One might wish to understand how different weighted and unweighted results are from each other (does weighting matter?) and be able to demonstrate that the weights applied are relevant to question(s) being asked.

In summary, a clear theoretical model or more simply a clear question that defines the purpose of the benchmarking exercise is essential. Recognize that multiple questions—purposes that the benchmarking results are to serve—raise complexity. Sometimes it would be better to have two or more models that are clearly relevant to the purpose specified. Parsimonious variable specification aids in creating results that are easier to interpret. Understand the limitations of proxy variables and be able to state why a proxy is a good measure for the underlying condition. Finally, understand the effects of weighting schemes; it might be, for instance, better to apply filters to unweighted results. In the next section, we attempt to show that many of the questions raised above can be answered empirically using multivariate statistical methods.

NEW DIRECTIONS FOR INSTITUTIONAL RESEARCH • DOI: 10.1002/ir

Figure 8.2. Group Identification

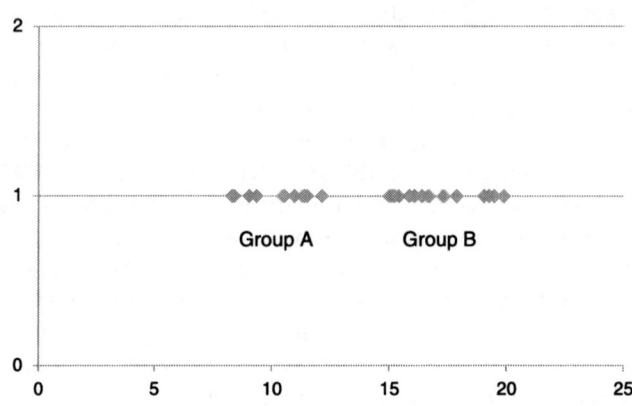

Taming Multivariate Data

The problem of finding clusters of observations in data sets can often be easily solved using graphical techniques. For example, consider the data shown in Figure 8.2.

Here, we have multiple cases where only a single variable has been measured for each case. It is clear, visually, that there are two groups in these data. In analyzing what we see, there are three noticeable outcomes. First, we notice that there is variability in the observed variable; the greater the variability, the greater the range of the variable and therefore the greater the ability to observe differences. Second, there are observations that are close to one another. Finally, there is a gap between the groups of observations that are close to one another.

Figure 8.3 shows a similar situation where we have multiple cases in which two variables have been measured for each case.

Visually, it is easy to see that there are three groups of cases. Again, we have high variability in each variable, cases that are close to each other, and gaps between the cases that are close to one another. Similar graphs could be drawn in three-dimensional space, but once the number of variables exceeds three, visual graphical methods fail.

When faced with a problem dependent on a large number of variables, it is common for researchers to try to reduce the dimensionality of the problem to something that they could possibly visualize. Further, since there may be a need to order individual data cases, often the dimensionality is reduced by creating a one-dimensional index of the form:

$$Index_j = \sum_{i=1}^{p} w_i x_{ij} \qquad (1)$$

Figure 8.3. Group Identification

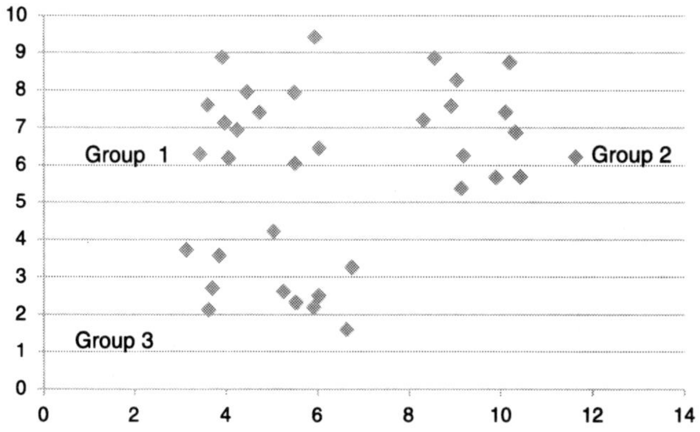

where the x_{ij} are the p values of the variables for individual case j, j varying from 1 to n, and the w_i are weights, usually subjectively chosen and often required to be non-negative. This reduction from p to one dimension is fraught with problems often overlooked by the index creators.

As a first example, assume the weights are required to add to 1 and are required to be non-negative. The weights then become proportions and are chosen to reflect the assumed relative importance of each variable. For example, one of the x variables might be the research expenditures of a university, and another might be the size of the student body. The first variable would be measured in millions of dollars, while the second would probably be measured in thousands. This means that combining them together in the index would give the research variable a contribution approximately *one thousand* times greater than the size variable. Accordingly, it is necessary to rescale the x variables so that the magnitude of the contribution to the index is not dominated by variables with large values. This is most simply accomplished by subtracting the variable sample mean and dividing the results by the variable standard deviation. This results in variables that all have a mean of 0 and a standard deviation of 1. More specifically, the equations for the transformation are:

$$z_{ij} = \frac{x_{ij} - \overline{x}_i}{s_i}, \tag{2}$$

where

$$\overline{x}_i = \frac{\sum_{j=1}^{n} x_{ij}}{n} \quad and \quad s_i^2 = \frac{\sum_{j=1}^{n} (x_{ij} - \overline{x}_i)^2}{n-1}$$

The new index, using the z scores, would now be of the form:

$$Index_j = \sum_{i=1}^{p} w_i z_{ij} \qquad (3)$$

Now that the variables are on an equal footing, the problem becomes how to choose the weights. Often, this is done subjectively, but there are objective criteria that may be applied. Examine the line drawn in Figure 8.4. By rotating the entire space by about 45 degrees, one arrives at Figure 8.5.

As can be seen, along the line where $y = 0$, the three groups overlap very little and are in order with Group 3 on the left, Group 1 in the middle, and Group 2 on the right. If one used the simple index:

$$Index_j = .5z_{1j} + .5z_{2j}$$

Figure 8.4. Possible Group Separating Line

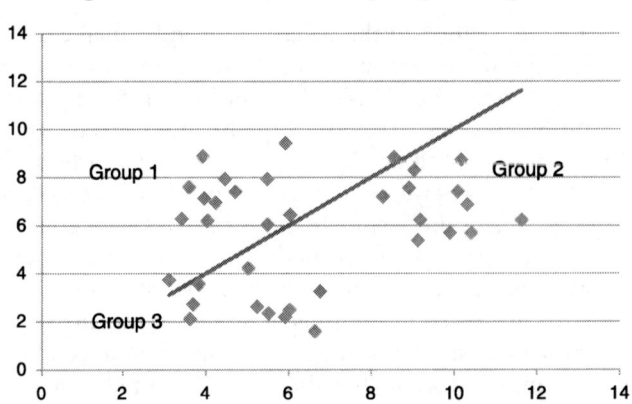

Figure 8.5. Rotated Group Separating Line

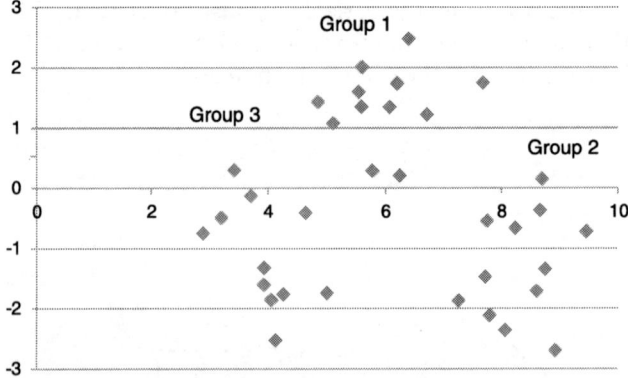

Figure 8.6. Rotated Group Separating Line

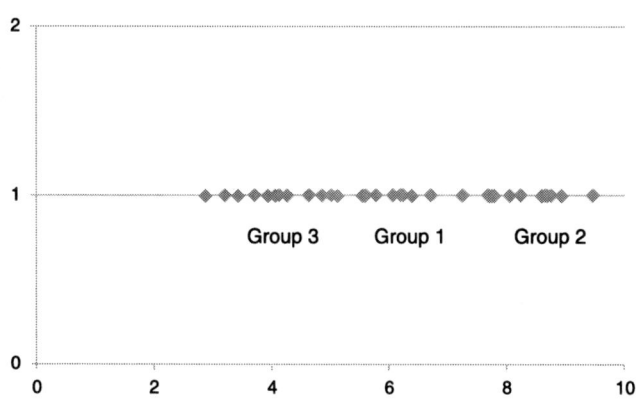

then this index would result in Figure 8.6, which shows how the groups could be identified.

The basis for choosing the index is related to a mathematical characteristic of the correlation matrix of the data. Let R be a $p \times p$ matrix with entry r_{ij} in row i and column j of the matrix. r_{ij} is the correlation between variable i and variable j in the data set with $r_{ii} = 1$ *for $i = 1, \ldots, p$*. Then the eigenvectors of the matrix R are defined as the p vectors $\underline{u}_i$ that have the property that:

$$R\underline{u}_i = \lambda_i \underline{u}_i \qquad (4)$$

The λ_i are called the eigenvalues associated with the eigenvectors.[4] If one wanted to construct a one-dimensional index that maximized the separation of the data points, then one would find the maximum eigenvalue and construct the index based on the eigenvector associated with it. This is basically the direction in p dimensional space that maximizes the range of the data. This eigenvector can be written as a linear combination of the original variables associated with each case, and therefore it is often possible to interpret the "meaning" of the eigenvector by examining the coefficients of the original variables that define it. An example of this will be given below.

A comparison of Figure 8.5 with Figure 8.6 shows that it is easier to interpret groups in Figure 8.5 than in Figure 8.6 due to the information provided by the second dimension. The eigenvector analysis can be continued by examining the eigenvectors with the two greatest values. The second eigenvector is a different linear combination of the original variables and has the desirable feature that the correlation between the two linear combinations is zero. Thus, whatever information is in the second eigenvector is uncorrelated with the information in the first eigenvector. This is important since often the original variables are highly correlated, making interpretation of effects extremely difficult. The process can be continued by taking the third, fourth, and so on eigenvectors, all of which are uncorrelated with each other. In fact, if one starts with p variables, one can extract up to p eigenvectors ordered from the largest to the smallest eigenvalues. This, however, results in a graphical situation as complicated as the original problem, with the only gain being that the new factors (eigenvectors) are uncorrelated. Accordingly, one desires to extract fewer than p factors, with the number of extracted factors much smaller than p. The most common method for determining the number of factors to be extracted is to focus only on factors with eigenvalues greater than 1. Since the variables have been converted to z-scores, this implies only using factors with variability greater than that found in a single variable (further justifications for this procedure may be found in Guttman, 1954, and Kaiser, 1960). Put another way, it excludes variables with low variability, less than that present in a single variable. Using fewer than the original p variables also mitigates the problems of which variables to use originally. If redundant variables are added, initially, the number of factors actually used is not highly affected.

Finally, it is important to try to get some understanding of the meaning of the factors chosen. Each factor can be expressed as a linear combination of the original p variables, and most computer programs supply the coefficients of the variables for each factor. However, since orientation of the points in space is not affected by rotation, usually various rotations of the data set are made to see if one can enhance the interpretation of the factors. The most common method used is the Varimax rotation, which for each factor tries to maximize the number of large (in absolute value) and small coefficients, hopefully making interpretation of the meaning of the factor easier.

To illustrate the above procedure consider a data set of 373 institutions for which the seven variables shown in Table 8.1 have been obtained.

High-cost programs are programs such as engineering, computer science, and so on, that require extensive laboratory space and laboratory equipment. The correlation matrix of these variables is given in Table 8.2 (only the lower half is shown since the upper half can be obtained by symmetry).

Table 8.1. Seven Variable Model

Identifier	Definition
V1	Total enrollment
V2	75th percentile score of freshmen
V3	Percentage of UG enrollment
V4	Percentage of full-time student enrollment
V5	Operating revenue per FTE student
V6	Average full professor salary
V7	Percentage of high-cost programs

Table 8.2. Seven Variable Model: Correlation Matrix

			Correlation Matrix			
	V1	V2	V3	V4	V5	V6	V7
V1	1.00						
V2	0.27	1.00					
V3	−0.31	−0.14	1.00				
V4	0.18	0.41	0.19	1.00			
V5	0.43	0.29	−0.48	0.26	1.00		
V6	0.65	0.40	−0.43	0.30	0.69	1.00	
V7	0.25	0.03	−0.22	−0.08	0.38	0.33	1.00

Table 8.3. Seven Variable Model: Eigenvalues

Identifier	Eigenvalue
V1	2.9606
V2	1.4200
V3	0.8163
V4	0.6625
V5	0.5962
V6	0.3258
V7	0.2286

Table 8.4. Seven Variable Model Factor Coefficients

Identifier	Factor 1 Coefficients	Factor 2 Coefficients
V1	0.64	0.36
V2	0.17	0.73
V3	−0.75	0.15
V4	−0.11	0.87
V5	0.76	0.35
V6	0.76	0.49
V7	0.63	−0.15

Using Proc FACTOR in the SAS Statistical Analysis System with the "Principal Components" option (Table 8.3), the seven eigenvalues were extracted (code for the SAS Programs referred to on the following page may be found in the Technical Appendix at the end of this chapter). This would indicate that only two factors are needed to analyze this data even though seven variables were originally included.

Finally, the rotated coefficients (the result of applying the VARIMAX option) of the two uncorrelated factors are given in Table 8.4. As can be seen, the factors have divided the variables into two groups (this does not always happen). The first factor puts positive weight on the variables V1 (total enrollment), V5 (Operating Revenue per FTE student), V6 (average salary of full professors), and V7 (percentage of high-cost programs) while putting negative weight on V3 (percentage of undergraduate enrollment). This pattern is consistent with large tier-one research institutions. One might call this factor "University Characteristics." The second factor puts positive weight on V2 (the 75th SAT percentile of the freshmen) and V4 (percentage of students who are full time). These are characteristics of the student population, so one might call this factor "Student Characteristics." Since the two factors are uncorrelated, we can see two easy-to-understand dimensions in this data set. It should be emphasized that it is not always the case that the factors partition the initial variables as nicely as in this example.

Most programs that perform the preceding analysis have an option to output the numerical values of the uncorrelated factors for each case. This would allow one, for example, to compute the distance between any two cases (the SAS procedure DISTANCE allows many different ways of doing this). So if you were interested in which universities were similar to your own, you could take the distances between your university and the others and order them to see which universities are close to your own. Alternatively, if you had a group of universities that your own university wished to emulate, you could compare the scores on the factors between your university and the aspiration universities to help in devoting resources to areas that would bring your institution closer to the aspirant group.

Finally, if you were interested in a visual display, then you could just use the factor scores to plot the cases in space if the number of factors was less than or equal to three. If more than three factors have been extracted, then you could use techniques like Multi-Dimensional Scaling (done in SAS with procedure MDS), which takes a matrix of differences between cases and maps it into the best one-, two-, or three-dimensional space, irrespective of how many factors were extracted.

The preceding procedure empirically reduces a complex multidimensional problem to a manageable size by reducing the number of interrelated variables to a more manageable number of uncorrelated factors that summarize the essential features of the original data set in a manner that facilitates understanding of the data and allows further analysis.

Notes

1. Each of the four components can and do change over time—the larger structural context—demographic, governmental, societal needs, and so on change over time; the quality of inputs vary; the processes (presumably) improve; and the outputs should thus be altered/improved/made consonant with larger demand.
2. Actually, as anyone doing a cursory search can discover, there is an entire industry offering an array of methods, products and "solutions," courses and certifications, and how-to manuals on how to recognize a "best practice," without reducing the whole process to absurdity.
3. Other stakeholders, such as faculty, may not like the outcomes and may use their special expertise to raise a host of research design, methodological, and variable specification issues.

NEW DIRECTIONS FOR INSTITUTIONAL RESEARCH • DOI: 10.1002/ir

4. A concise introduction to the ideas can be found at http://en.widipedia.org/wiki/
Eigenvectors.

Technical Appendix

All code is given for SAS Version 9.2.

The first SAS program performs the principal component analysis and extracts the eigenvectors with eigenvalues greater than 1.0.

```
PROC FACTOR DATA = SCHOOLS
SIMPLE
METHOD = PRIN
PRIORS = ONE
MINEIGEN = 1
SCREE
ROTATE = VARIMAX
ROUND
CORR
FLAG = .4    NFACTORS = 2    OUT = WORK.FACTORS;
VAR V1–V7;
RUN;
```

V1–V7 represent our seven variables discussed earlier.

The output factors are input for the proc distance procedure below.

The second SAS program computes the distance of each case from every other case using the factors created by the first program.

```
PROC DISTANCE DATA = FACTORS OUT = FACTORS1
SHAPE = SQUARE
METHOD = EUCLID;
VAR INTERVAL(FACTOR1-FACTOR2/STD = STD);
ID NAME;
RUN;
```

NAME is the variable that contains the name of the case (school).

If the number of factors chosen is three or greater, the following SAS procedure takes the distances computed by the above program, and plots the cases in the "best" fitting two-dimensional space. It was not used in the example above since we only extracted two factors.

```
PROC MDS DATA = FACTORS1
RANDOM = 123
LEVEL = ABSOLUTE
OUT = JW(WHERE = (_TYPE_ = 'CONFIG'));
ID NAME;
RUN;
```

References

Borden V.M.H. "Identifying and Analyzing Group Differences." In M. A. Coughlin (ed.), *Applications of Intermediate/Advanced Statistics in Institutional Research.* Tallahassee, Fla.: Association for Institutional Research, 2005.

Carnegie Foundation for the Advancement of Teaching. Carnegie Classifications Data File, February, 2012. Retrieved February 23, 2012, from http://classifications.carnegiefoundation.org/resources/.

Guttman, L. "Some Necessary and Sufficient Conditions for the Common Factor Analysis." *Psychometrika,* 1954, *19,* 149–161.

Kaiser, H. F. "The Application of Electronic Computers to Factor Analysis." *Educational and Psychological Measurement,* 1960, *20,* 141–151.

Knapp, L. G., Kelly-Reid, J. E., and Ginder, S. A. *Enrollment in Postsecondary Institutions, Fall 2010; Financial Statistics, Fiscal Year 2010; and Graduation Rates, Selected Cohorts, 2002–07* (NCES 2012–280). U.S. Department of Education. Washington, D.C.: National Center for Education Statistics, 2012. Retrieved June 20 2012, from http://www.eric.ed.gov/PDFS/ED530514.pdf.

Merrill, T., and Stanley, J. "An Evidence-Based Strategy for Selecting Peer Institutions." Presentation at the PacAIR Annual Meeting, November 19, 2010.

Teeter, D. J., and Brinkman, P. T. "Peer Institutional Studies/Institutional Comparisons." In J. A. Muffo and G. W. McLaughlin (eds.), *A Primer on Institutional Research.* Tallahassee, Fla.: Association for Institutional Research, 1987.

Teeter, D. J., and Brinkman, P. T. "Peer Institutions." In M. A. Whiteley, J. D. Porter, and R. H. Fenske (eds.), *The Primer on Institutional Research.* Tallahassee, Fla.: Association for Institutional Research, 1992.

Teeter, D. J., and Christal, M. E. "A Comparison of Procedures for Establishing Peer Groups." Paper presented at the Annual Meeting of the Southern Association for Institutional Research, 1984.

Terenzini, P. T., Hartmark, L., Lorang, W. G., and Shirley, R. C. "A Conceptual and Methodological Approach to the Identification of Peer Institutions." *Research in Higher Education,* 1980, *12*(4), 347–364.

Trainer, J. "The Role of Institutional Research in Conducting Comparative Analysis of Peers." In D. G. Terkla (ed.), *Institutional Research: More than Just Data.* New Directions for Higher Education (no. 141, pp. 21–30). San Francisco: Jossey-Bass, 2008.

Weeks, S. F., Puckett, D., and Daron, R. "Developing Peer Groups for the Oregon University System: From Politics to Analysis (and Back)." *Research in Higher Education,* 2000, *41*(1), 1–20.

Wheeler, S. "The Structure of Formally Organized Socialization Settings." In O. G. Brim Jr. and S. Wheeler (eds.), *Socialization After Childhood: Two Essays.* New York: John Wiley & Sons, 1966, 53–116.

LAWRENCE J. REDLINGER *is the Executive Director of the Office of Strategic Planning and Analysis and a Professor of Sociology at the University of Texas at Dallas.*

JOHN J. WIORKOWSKI *is Vice Provost and Professor of Statistics at the University of Texas at Dallas.*

ANNA I. MOSES *is a Senior Institutional Research Associate in the Office of Strategic Planning and Analysis at the University of Texas at Dallas.*

9

This chapter summarizes some significant information from the eight preceding chapters.

Conclusions and Future Directions

Fred Lillibridge

It is my pleasure to write the concluding chapter in this very useful addition to the institutional research literature. Benchmarking, when done properly, offers a lot of promise for higher education units that want to improve how they do business. It is clear that much is known, but still more needs to be learned before it reaches its full potential as a useful tool. The reader has been treated to useful and down-to-earth approaches to very sophisticated statistical methodologies. My goal in this chapter is to hit the high spots and topics I found most interesting as I read the unique chapters.

Where It All Began

Sharron L. Ronco and Gary D. Levy introduce the concept of benchmarking and how higher education institutions began to use benchmarking for a variety of purposes in Chapter 1, "How Benchmarking and Higher Education Came Together." They point out that the origin of the term *benchmarking* is not known. Benchmarking practitioners use standards or references to measure, compare, or judge how well the process is operating compared to processes and/or outcomes either within the organizations or in an external organization. The goal is to improve existing processes and/or outcomes and provide a metric for future comparisons.

Benchmarking in business started in the 1970s when Xerox discovered that it could not compete with Japanese copier manufacturers. Xerox examined each operation in the competitors' copier production process.

What they learned was used to make their design and production more efficient, which allowed them to reduce manufacturing expenses and be more profitable.

The authors next discussed various innovations in the development of benchmarking. The first was cross-industry benchmarking. This method focused on how well a process was done and not just on the quality of the product or service rendered. The next innovation was the start of the quality movement in the 1990s. This approach emphasized benchmarking as an effective way to assess and improve quality within the organization. Next, there was the Continuous Quality Improvement approach that emerged from Total Quality Management. This approach looked within an organization to determine the level of quality being produced. These data were then used to establish improvement targets. Benchmarking reached a significant milestone when the Malcolm Baldrige National Quality Award was authorized by Congress in 1988. The focus for this award was identifying best practices and improvements in organization quality. The Baldrige award framework established criteria that have driven the national quality improvement agenda and led to the creation of state quality awards. Clearly, benchmarking has had a positive impact on business and industry, but how about in higher education?

I'm reminded about an old higher education joke. It went something like this: How many professors does it take to change a light bulb? Answer: *Change?* In the 1990s, some in higher education saw benchmarking as a way to cope with this resistance to change.

Despite the potential benefits, full-scale benchmarking has been undertaken by a relatively small number of higher education institutions. One reason offered is that some use performance indicators and performance funding as if it was appropriate for benchmarking. This approach fails to grasp that benchmarking is about improving processes, not just counting things.

There are a variety of benchmarking types. These include internal benchmarking, external benchmarking, competitive benchmarking, and functional benchmarking. More recent types include best-in-class or generic benchmarking. Each has its own unique purposes. Higher education tends to rely on metric, or performance, benchmarking to use quantified data to evaluate relative performance. Process benchmarking relies on the time-consuming identification of best practices to improve performance. Diagnostic benchmarking performs a continuous "health check" of both practice and performance.

Higher education's use of benchmarking is evidenced by applications used by organizations like the National Association of College and University Business Officers (NACUBO) and the University of Delaware's Delaware Study beginning in 1990s. Other large-scale benchmarking endeavors include: the National Community College Benchmark Project (NCCBP), the Voluntary System of Accountability, and the Individual Development and Educational Assessment (IDEA) Center. The National Center for Education Statistics (NCES) has developed many useful peer comparison tools. Educational Benchmarking, Inc. (EBI) also provides useful benchmarking resources.

Internationally, benchmarking is seen as a way to deal with public and governmental concerns. The United Kingdom has used benchmarking since the 1980s. Australia, New Zealand, Canada, Germany, and other European nations have more recently become involved in the benchmarking movement. The Bologna Process has been used to benchmark disciplinary learning outcomes and create comparable and compatible quality assurance and academic degree standards.

The authors suggest that written accounts of full-scale higher education benchmarking efforts are difficult to find. They offer some possible reasons why higher education has been slow to adopt. I think the notion of benchmarking best practices appeals to almost everyone. The difficulty comes in finding reliable data to measure performance of what are really educational constructs that do not lend themselves to quantification. The authors conclude that "benchmarking activities in higher education have now been firmly established and accepted, as institutions seek to improve the quality and efficiency of the many activities in which they are engaged." I agree.

Practical Uses of Higher Education Benchmarking

In Chapter 2, "Internal Benchmarking for Institutional Effectiveness," Sharron Ronco discusses the application of benchmarking processes within higher education institutions. The purpose of benchmarking is to identify the processes that utilize best practices that lead to sustained improved performance. Effective benchmarking in its purest form is not prevalent in higher education. However, internal benchmarking has worked because it avoids issues like access, cooperation, comparability, and transferability of processes across institutions. Internal benchmarking looks within an organization to find best in-house practices and then share lessons learned with other groups in the organization. Some examples where higher education has effectively used this form of benchmarking include admissions, hiring, assessment of student learning outcomes, approaches to strategic planning, academic and administrative support services, and delivery of online instruction. To be effective, institutions must acknowledge that they can improve their processes, and they must have at least two similar processes in the organization to compare.

Ronco offers a guide to conducting an internal benchmarking study that provides questions that need to be answered to plan the study, collect and analyze information, and implement change. The first step is to identify critical areas in need of improvement. The last is to summarize their findings and communicate them to appropriate audiences and make recommendations about how to use the best-practice standards they discovered. It is also critical that the implementation process be monitored and assessed to see if improvement is sustained. Looking inward allows an institution to better understand how it operates, and it is an important step to eventually comparing its processes to the best practices used in other organizations. Internal benchmarking can help demonstrate a commitment to improvement.

In Chapter 3, "Benchmarking and Enrollment Management," Robert L. Duniway offers a variety of approaches for using benchmarking to manage enrollment and suggests ways to construct a process for improving enrollment management. All higher education institutions recruit and enroll new students and work to help them complete their educational programs. The enrollment management process includes such things as prospecting, applications received, admit rates, yield, financial aid discounting, retention, graduation rates, academic progress efficiency, and managing course section offerings—all that can be should be assessed by using benchmarking techniques. Managed enrollment has revenue implications. Key metrics include total revenue (net institutional financial aid) and the marginal cost per additional student of providing instruction and other services.

A sound approach is to benchmark against a set of carefully selected peer institutions. Finding institutions that are similar to yours can be very difficult. Finding and gaining access to comparable data is a key to success. Even with these limitations, benchmarking can be useful. Finding good peer institutions and gaining access to their data can be difficult, although there are still ways, like using internal benchmarks that can be used to compare your institution with others. Historical performance and trends on key enrollment metrics among internal units can also be compared.

Enrollment management can be viewed as a longitudinal process that focuses on stages of admission and retention and graduation rates. But there are other critical aspects that need to be considered. An admission stage funnel is offered as a graphical depiction of student admissions. At the top are recruited potential students or prospects. The number of prospects who inquire or respond is used to calculate a response rate. Potential students who complete the application are used to compute a conversion rate. The number who are finally admitted is used to calculate an admit rate. Gross yield and melt rates are calculated using the number of students who confirm or make deposits and those who finally enroll. Tracking individuals through the funnel will result in critical data for enrollment management.

Finding comparable data to benchmark against can be challenging. Good sources include the Integrated Postsecondary Education Data System (IPEDS), the Common Data Set (CDS), Noel-Levitz, Peterson's, or U.S. News. Where external data are not available or scarce, institutions can look at which strategies provide the best or worst return on investment.

Financial aid data can be used in a variety of ways. The data can be used to target potential students. The NCES College Navigator website makes it easy to access the average net price of peer institutions and average net price for family income ranges. IPEDS data can be helpful in estimating discount rates and average net tuition and fees per student.

Student academic success is what really matters. This is achieved by passing courses that lead to completion awards. IPEDS retention and graduation rates provide benchmarking data that measures this activity. This data can be supplemented with transfer data from the National Student Data Clearinghouse matching service. The author suggests a variety of other ways to look at student progress and success.

A key to effectively using enrollment management benchmark data is evaluating how comparable the data is. How these comparisons are made will affect the usefulness of the data. Understanding your data and data about other institutions is critical to the effort. The selection of peers can be helped by using IPEDS data and analysis tools. Where apples-to-apples comparisons are not possible, the researcher must be careful to understand the limits of the data and appropriateness of the comparisons. Depending on the criticalness of the decision, it is often true that good is good enough.

Institutions will sometimes find that no matter how hard they look, it might not be possible to find reasonable external benchmark data. Subpopulations and historical performance are internal reference groups that can be useful when other data are not available. The chapter concludes that enrollment management is a complex activity and benchmarking will help the institution focus on critical issues.

In Chapter 4, "Using Institutional Survey Data to Jump-Start Your Benchmarking Process," Timothy Chow discusses the use of survey data to determine institutions for competitive benchmarking purposes. Institutions expend large amounts of staff time completing surveys. Using those surveys to improve internal practices helps mitigate this vast expenditure of time and opportunity costs. Institutional surveys can be useful to help select potential peers or best processes. While all kinds of institutional surveys are conducted, one of the most important is the IPEDS data collection. Organizations that conduct other common institutional surveys include the American Association of University Professors (AAUP), the Council for Aid to Education (CAE), the College and University Professional Association for Human Resources (CUPA-HR), the National Association of Colleges and Employers (NACE), the National Association of College and University Business Officers (NACUBO), and the National Science Foundation (NSF).

There are also others that are widely used, including the National Survey of Student Engagement (NSSE) and the Cooperative Institutional

Research Project (CIRP). Other good sources of data can come from resource groups like the Carnegie Foundation for the Advancement of Teaching, the Higher Education Data Sharing (HEDS) consortium, the Association of American Universities Data Exchange (AAUDE), Southern Universities Group (SUG), and the Consortium for Student Retention Data Exchange (CSRDE).

Researchers can compose a "super" index of average rankings of many performance criteria. Multiple-criteria decision making (MCDM) or multiple-criteria decision analysis (MCDA) can be used when appropriate. Researchers must be aware that institutional surveys have limitations. Surveys tend to focus on the institutional level and not the discipline level. Survey results are often out of date and survey items may change, making it difficult to use for comparisons. If possible, multiple sources should be used to triangulate and verify results. Data exchange groups or consortia can also be excellent sources for data.

This Could Really Work

In Chapter 5, "Learning How to Play Ball: Applying Sabermetric Thinking to Benchmarking in Higher Education," Gary Levy provides a brief overview of baseball sabermetric thinking and demonstrates a simple application of sabermetric methods to benchmarking in a higher education context. I think it provides a very creative treatment about how approaches used in baseball to assess the value of players can be retooled to work for higher education. My first experience with statistics began when I was six years old, when I began to chart my little league batting average. This was a great read even if you were never a baseball junkie.

Baseball uses sabermetric thinking and methodologies to assess effectiveness. These techniques may be useful for higher education benchmarking. *Sabermetrics* is a term created specifically for baseball. It deals with using math and statistics to develop and add knowledge about baseball. Sabermetrics, like benchmarking, is designed to replace traditional intuitive and inward-looking approaches with more rigorous analytic and quantitative methods.

A modest application of sabermetric thinking to higher education benchmarking is offered. Faculty members can be considered as the players. Basic metrics could include simple counts as class sections taught (CT), total student credit hours generated (SCH), students advised (SA), peer-refereed publications (RP), nonrefereed publications (NRP), contracts and grants submitted (CGS), contracts and grants awarded (CGA), and contract and grant award dollars (CGA$).

Success in baseball is scoring more runs and winning the game. Success in higher education is not as clear. Success is a construct composed of many factors and in many domains. The identification of these factors and domains is like selecting performance indicators in traditional benchmarking.

While the examples presented deal only with financial data, it is possible to use these sabermetric methodologies on other data. Researchers could use a count approach to count the number of classes taught, number of student credits (SCH) generated, and number of contracts and grants awarded. As in baseball, ratio or quotient methodologies could be used to provide simple descriptions of the efficiency and productivity for each faculty member. It might even be possible to develop an academic version of slugging average. While this approach offers a new way of benchmarking, in the end decision makers must use objective and subjective information, judgment, and intuition.

Finding Benchmark Peers

In Chapter 6, "Selecting Peer Institutions with IPEDS and Other Nationally Available Data," Sarah Carrigan discusses how institutions can use IPEDS data to assist their institutions in determining what other institutions should be used in external benchmark analysis. A case study is used to show how to select national data sources that can be used to identify potential peers. The following sources are presented: IPEDS, the NCES Library Statistics program, CUPA-HR, and the Carnegie Classification of Institutions of Higher Education. The chapter features a web-based peer selection tool (PST) that is used to select institutional peers.

Data used in the selection tool came from the NCES nationwide library statistics program. The Academic Libraries Survey data can be accessed using a website that allows users to create reports that compare libraries using selected data elements. CUPA-HR conducts annual compensation and salary surveys and publishes national mean and median salary data. Institutions can also subscribe to DataOnDemand to obtain direct access to surveys.

The Carnegie Foundation for the Advancement of Teaching produces the Carnegie Classification of Institutions of Higher Education. This classification system allows operational and benchmark comparisons. These disparate data sources could easily be merged to build larger data sets containing a wide variety of data points.

The University of North Carolina General Administration (UNC-GA) developed a web-based PST to meet the peer selection requirement. Data from the entire 2009–10 collection cycle was used to create seventy comparison variables. Institutions can control variable weights. The PST uses a weighted distance index to rank all comparison institutions in relation to the target institution. An example of how institutional stakeholders and leaders used the PST during the peer selection process is presented. It describes a deliberative decision process and the role of the director of institutional research.

NEW DIRECTIONS FOR INSTITUTIONAL RESEARCH • DOI: 10.1002/ir

Benchmarking Town and Gown

In Chapter 7, "Benchmarking Tier-One Universities: 'Keeping Up with the Joneses,'" Nicolas A. Valcik, Kimberly Scruton, Stuart Murchison, Ted Benavides, Todd Jordan, Andrea Stigdon, and Angela Olszewski explore whether a link exists between public top-tier institutions and their host municipalities. The study then looks at whether the same link exists in the state of Texas's "Emerging Universities." The *U.S. News and World Report* (USNWR) "America's Best College" ranking system has influenced U.S. institutions to try to move up to the top tier. State legislation to reward improved rankings has also become law. This happened in Texas in 2009 when increased funding was offered to seven public emerging universities if they earned a top-tier ranking. Not much has been published about the connection between city services and university tier-one status.

A case is made that better universities provide top-performing students who become well educated and desired by businesses needing highly skilled employees. Many city administrators believe that a top-tier higher education institution, because of its high reputation, can benefit their city in many ways. Institutional research offices can analyze the institution and host city relationship. It may only be necessary to add municipal data to the office's existing data. Key research questions were analyzed. Is the economy in small cities more dependent on a university than a bigger city would be? Do small cities tend to be more connected with their university with joint city–university programs? Can a good relationship with the city help the university improve its USNWR rankings? The answers to these questions were applied to seven "emerging" Texas public research universities to see whether host municipality characteristics can predict success in attaining top-tier status.

Researchers found a correlation between public top-tier universities and their host municipalities. Economic benefits are realized when cities and top-tier public universities work together. Working with host cities may allow emerging universities to save resources that can be used to make the changes necessary to get tier-one status. For instance, a university may use the money they saved to increase salaries. Then faculty will pay more taxes that can be used in the city to make schools better and provide amenities that will attract businesses and increased population. Like the adage that "the rich get richer," it may also be true that a high-quality and high-reputation university and their host city will both benefit in the relationship.

The Path Less Traveled

In Chapter 8, "Taming Multivariate Data: Conceptual and Methodological Issues," Lawrence J. Redlinger, John J. Wiorkowski, and Anna I. Moses discuss the methodological and statistical challenges in selecting appropriate

NEW DIRECTIONS FOR INSTITUTIONAL RESEARCH • DOI: 10.1002/ir

peer institutions for benchmarking. An impressive and extensive review of the literature that surrounds higher education benchmarking is provided. This chapter is a hard-core statistician's dream. It might be too much for the novice benchmarker.

Like most of the other chapters, the goal of this work is to select appropriate peer institutions. A number of statistical models are presented. The subject of this research is students and other people who are more difficult to study than the production of widgets. Students have personal agendas that interact with higher education processes.

The researchers use IPEDS data to determine what to include in the study. Institutions are classified with the Carnegie Foundation for the Advancement of Teaching data. The study question will dictate which institutions to include. The goal is to "establish a set of similar institutions based on a set of characteristics that allow for comparisons at a point in time or over a defined time period." The question also drives the decision about which variables to choose. These variables would be environmental, structural, or contextual. Researchers select variables for a clear purpose and not add additional variables that might be highly correlated with each other. Analysis with fewer measures may be easier to interpret. Proxy measures should be used with care. If weighting variables is being considered, the analysis should be run with and without the weights to see how the results are affected.

The authors present an impressive array of graphical clustering techniques. When many variables are being studied, it might be better to visualize the data.

The collected works presented in this volume will be very useful for researchers who want a survey of benchmarking and practical techniques for doing it.

FRED LILLIBRIDGE *is the Associate Vice President of Institutional Effectiveness and Planning at Doña Ana Community College.*

NEW DIRECTIONS FOR INSTITUTIONAL RESEARCH • DOI: 10.1002/ir

INDEX

OTHER TITLES AVAILABLE IN THE
NEW DIRECTIONS FOR INSTITUTIONAL RESEARCH SERIES
Paul D. Umbach, Editor-in-Chief

IR 155   **Refining the Focus on Faculty Diversity in Postsecondary Institutions**
Yonghong Jade Xu
Faculty diversity is gaining unprecedented emphasis in the mission of
colleges and universities, and institutional researchers are being pushed for
relevant data. In this volume, six chapters examine faculty diversity from a
variety of perspectives. Together, they constitute a comprehensive outlook
on the subject, highlighting factors including racial background, gender,
citizenship, employment status, and academic discipline, and examining
how growing diversity has aff ected the work experience and productivity of
faculty and the learning outcomes of students. Special attention is given to
international and nontenure-track faculty members, two groups that have
experienced rapid growth in recent years. Chapter authors present empirical
evidence to support the increasing importance of faculty diversity in
institutional research, to show the need for actively tracking the changes in
diversity over time, and to highlight the critical role of research methodology
in all such work.
ISBN: 978-1-1185-2675-0

IR 154   **Multilevel Modeling Techniques and Applications in Institutional Research**
Joe L. Lott, II, and James S. Antony
Multilevel modeling is an increasingly popular multivariate technique that
is widely applied in the social sciences. Increasingly, institutional research
(IR) practitioners are making instructional decisions based on results from
their multivariate analyses, which often come from nested data that lend
themselves to multilevel modeling techniques. As colleges and universities
continue to face mounting pressures to shrink their budgets and maximize
resources while at the same time maintaining and even increasing their
institutional profiles, data-driven decision making will be critical. Multilevel
modeling is one tool that will lead to more efficient estimates and enhance
understanding of complex relationships.
      The express purpose of this volume of *New Directions for Institutional
Research* is to illustrate both the theoretical underpinnings and practical
applications of multilevel modeling in IR. Chapters in this volume introduce
the fundamental concepts of multilevel modeling techniques in both a
conceptual and technical manner. Authors provide a range of examples of
nested models that are based on linear and categorical outcomes, and then
offer important suggestions about presenting results of multilevel models
through charts and graphs.
ISBN: 978-1-1184-4400-9

IR 153   **Data Use in the Community College**
Christopher M. Mullin, Trudy Bers, and Linda Serra Hagedorn
American community colleges represent a true success story. With their
multiple missions, they have provided access and opportunity to millions
of students who would not have otherwise had the opportunity to gain a
college degree, certificate, or technical training. But community colleges
are held accountable for their services and must be able to show that they
are indeed serving their variety of students appropriately. Providing that
evidence is the responsibility of the institutional research office, which must

function not only as the data collection point but also as the decipherer of the story the different types of data tell.

This volume speaks of the multiplicity of data required to tell the community college story. The authors explore and detail how various sources—workforce data, market data, state-level data, federal data, and, of course, institutional data such as transcript files—all have something to say about the life of a community college. Much like an orchestral score, where the different parts played by individual instruments become music under the hands of a conductor, these data can be coordinated and assembled into a message that answers questions of student success and institutional effectiveness.

ISBN: 978-1-1183-8807-5

IR 152   **Attracting and Retaining Women in STEM**
Joy Gaston Gayles
Underrepresentation of women in science, technology, engineering, and mathematics fields is a problem that has persisted over the past three decades and is most severe at the highest levels of the STEM career path. Although national attention has been directed toward increasing the presence of women in STEM, women continue to leave at critical junctures in STEM training and careers at a higher rate than men. This volume of *New Directions for Institutional Research* takes a comprehensive look at the status of women in STEM and considers related factors, theoretical perspectives, and innovative tools that have the potential to help scholars understand, study, and improve the experiences of women in STEM fields.

ISBN: 978-1-1182-9769-8

IR 151   **Using Mixed-Methods Approaches to Study Intersectionality in Higher Education**
Kimberly A. Griffin, Samuel D. Museus
This volume of *New Directions for Institutional Research* focuses on using mixed-methods approaches and intersectionality frameworks in higher education research. The authors draw on intersectionality as a foundational theory for framing questions and interpreting results and discuss the importance of using a variety of methods to get useful, deep, honest answers from college faculty and students. They provide several examples of how such broad perspectives enhance the quality of scholarly and institutional research on faculty experiences and relationships, the challenges faced by faculty of color, college access and equity, privilege in higher education, campus climate research and assessment, and multiracial college students' experiences.

ISBN: 978-1-1181-7347-3

IR 150   **Validity and Limitations of College Student Self-Report Data**
Serge Herzog, Nicholas A. Bowman
Higher education administrators, institutional researchers (IR), and scholars rely heavily on the survey responses of college students, not least to meet mounting accountability pressures to document student learning and institutional effectiveness. However, research on the accuracy of students' self-reported learning, development, and experiences is quite limited. To address this critical issue, *Validity and Limitations of College Student Self-Report Data* provides seven empirical studies that examine the validity, use, and interpretation of such data, with an emphasis on student self-reported gains. The chapters are written by leading scholars in the field of college student self-reports, and they provide IR practitioners several analytical frameworks to gauge the accuracy of student survey data. The cumulative findings from this volume suggest that self-reported gains exhibit some significant biases, and they often do not constitute an adequate proxy for

longitudinal measures of learning and development. Still, student self-reports offer important subjective impressions about learning and affective development that may complement direct measures of outcomes, together yielding a more comprehensive picture of the college experience.
ISBN: 978-1-1181-3416-0

IR 149   **Assessing Complex General Education Student Learning Outcomes**
Jeremy D. Penn
One of the greatest challenges in assessing student learning in general education programs is addressing the tension between selecting easy-to-measure learning outcomes that have little value or bearing on our institutions' goals and selecting meaningful and substantial learning outcomes that are complex and difficult to assess. Many institutions that have recently replaced their cafeteria-style general education programs with general education programs that focus on complex student learning outcomes find themselves at a loss in attempting to gather evidence on student achievement of these outcomes for internal improvement and external accountability purposes.

This volume of *New Directions for Institutional Research* makes a compelling case that institutions can and should be assessing consequential, complex general education student learning outcomes. It also gives faculty members and assessment leaders the tools and resources to take ownership of this important work. Part One of this volume provides an argument for why we should be assessing general education and describes a framework, based on a rigorous psychological research approach, for engaging in assessment. The six chapters in Part Two show how this work can be (and is being) done for six important learning outcomes: critical thinking, quantitative reasoning, teamwork, intercultural competence, civic knowledge and engagement, and integrative learning. The volume closes with recommendations on needed innovations in general education assessment and presents a research agenda for future work.
ISBN: 978-1-1180-9133-3

IR 148   **Students of Color in STEM**
Shaun R. Harper, Christopher B. Newman
Why are some racial minorities so underrepresented as degree candidates in science, technology, engineering, and mathematics (STEM)? Why are they so underprepared for college-level math and science courses? Why are their grades and other achievement indicators disproportionately lower than their white counterparts? Why do so many of them change their majors to non-STEM fields? And why do so few pursue graduate degrees in STEM? These five questions are continuously recycled in the study of students of color in STEM. Offered in this volume of *New Directions for Institutional Research* are new research ideas and frameworks that have emerged from recent studies of minorities in STEM fields across a wide array of institution types: large research universities, community colleges, minority-serving institutions, and others. The chapter authors counterbalance examinations of student underperformance and racial disparities in STEM with insights into the study of factors that enable minority student success.
ISBN: 978-1-1180-1402-8

NEW DIRECTIONS FOR INSTITUTIONAL RESEARCH
ORDER FORM SUBSCRIPTION AND SINGLE ISSUES

DISCOUNTED BACK ISSUES:

Use this form to receive 20% off all back issues of *New Directions for Institutional Research*.
All single issues priced at **$23.20** (normally $29.00)

TITLE	ISSUE NO.	ISBN
_____	_____	_____
_____	_____	_____
_____	_____	_____

Call 888-378-2537 or see mailing instructions below. When calling, mention the promotional code JBNND to receive your discount. For a complete list of issues, please visit www.josseybass.com/go/ndir

SUBSCRIPTIONS: (1 YEAR, 4 ISSUES)

☐ New Order ☐ Renewal

U.S.	☐ Individual: $89	☐ Institutional: $297
CANADA/MEXICO	☐ Individual: $89	☐ Institutional: $337
ALL OTHERS	☐ Individual: $113	☐ Institutional: $371

Call 888-378-2537 or see mailing and pricing instructions below.
Online subscriptions are available at www.onlinelibrary.wiley.com

ORDER TOTALS:

Issue / Subscription Amount: $ _____

Shipping Amount: $ _____
(for single issues only – subscription prices include shipping)

Total Amount: $ _____

SHIPPING CHARGES:

First Item	$6.00
Each Add'l Item	$2.00

(No sales tax for U.S. subscriptions. Canadian residents, add GST for subscription orders. Individual rate subscriptions must be paid by personal check or credit card. Individual rate subscriptions may not be resold as library copies.)

BILLING & SHIPPING INFORMATION:

☐ **PAYMENT ENCLOSED:** *(U.S. check or money order only. All payments must be in U.S. dollars.)*

☐ **CREDIT CARD:** ☐ VISA ☐ MC ☐ AMEX

Card number _____ Exp. Date _____

Card Holder Name _____ Card Issue # _____

Signature _____ Day Phone _____

☐ **BILL ME:** *(U.S. institutional orders only. Purchase order required.)*

Purchase order # _____
Federal Tax ID 13559302 • GST 89102-8052

Name _____

Address _____

Phone _____ E-mail _____

Copy or detach page and send to: **John Wiley & Sons, One Montgomery Street, Suite 1200, San Francisco, CA 94104-4594**

Order Form can also be faxed to: **888-481-2665**

PROMO JBNND

Statement of Ownership

Statement of Ownership, Management, and Circulation (required by 39 U.S.C. 3685), filed on OCTOBER 1, 2012, for NEW DIRECTIONS FOR INSTITUTIONAL RESEARCH (Publication No. 0271-0579), published quarterly for an annual subscription price of $89 at Wiley Subscription Services, Inc... at Jossey-Bass, One Montgomery St., Suite 1200, San Francisco, CA 94104-4594.

The names and complete mailing addresses of the Publisher, Editor, and Managing Editor are: Publisher, Wiley Subscription Services, Inc., A Wiley Company at San Francisco, One Montgomery St., Suite 1200, San Francisco, CA 94104-4594; Editor, Paul Umbach, North Carolina State University, Raleigh, NC 27695; Managing Editor, Robert Rosenberg, Wiley Subscription Services Inc., One Montgomery St., Suite 1200, San Francisco, CA 94104-4594. Contact Person: Joe Schuman; Telephone: 415-782-3232.

NEW DIRECTIONS FOR INSTITUTIONAL RESEARCH is a publication owned by Wiley Subscription Services, Inc. The known bondholders, mortgagees, and other security holders owning or holding 1% or more of total amount of bonds, mortgages, or other securities are (see list).

	Average No. Copies Each Issue During Preceding 12 Months	No. Copies Of Single Issue Published Nearest To Filing Date (Summer 2012)		Average No. Copies Each Issue During Preceding 12 Months	No. Copies Of Single Issue Published Nearest To Filing Date (Summer 2012)
15a. Total number of copies (net press run)	807	814	15d(2). In-county nonrequested copies stated on PS form 3541	0	0
15b. Legitimate paid and/or requested distribution (by mail and outside mail)			15d(3). Nonrequested copies distributed through the USPS by other classes of mail	0	0
15b(1). Individual paid/requested mail subscriptions stated on PS form 3541 (include direct written request from recipient, telemarketing, and Internet requests from recipient, paid subscriptions including nominal rate subscriptions, advertiser's proof copies, and exchange copies)	256	197	15d(4). Nonrequested copies distributed outside the mail	0	0
			15e. Total nonrequested distribution (sum of 15d(1), (2), (3), and (4))	56	55
			15f. Total distribution (sum of 15c and 15e)	312	252
15b(2). Copies requested by employers for distribution to employees by name or position, stated on PS form 3541	0	0	15g. Copies not distributed	495	562
			15h. Total (sum of 15f and 15g)	807	814
15b(3). Sales through dealers and carriers, street vendors, counter sales, and other paid or requested distribution outside USPS	0	0	15i. Percent paid and/or requested circulation (15c divided by 15f times 100)	82.1%	78.1%
15b(4). Requested copies distributed by other mail classes through USPS	0	0			
15c. Total paid and/or requested circulation (sum of 15b(1), (2), (3), and (4))	256	197			
15d. Nonrequested distribution (by mail and outside mail)					
15d(1). Outside county nonrequested copies stated on PS form 3541	56	55			

I certify that all information furnished on this form is true and complete. I understand that anyone who furnishes false or misleading information on this form or who omits material or information requested on this form may be subject to criminal sanctions (including fines and imprisonment) and/or civil sanctions (including civil penalties).

Statement of Ownership will be printed in the Winter 2012 issue of this publication.

(signed) Susan E. Lewis, VP & Publisher-Periodicals

Lightning Source UK Ltd.
Milton Keynes UK
UKOW02f2305231214

243626UK00001B/39/P